AF575407

CONSTABLE'S
WHITE HORSE

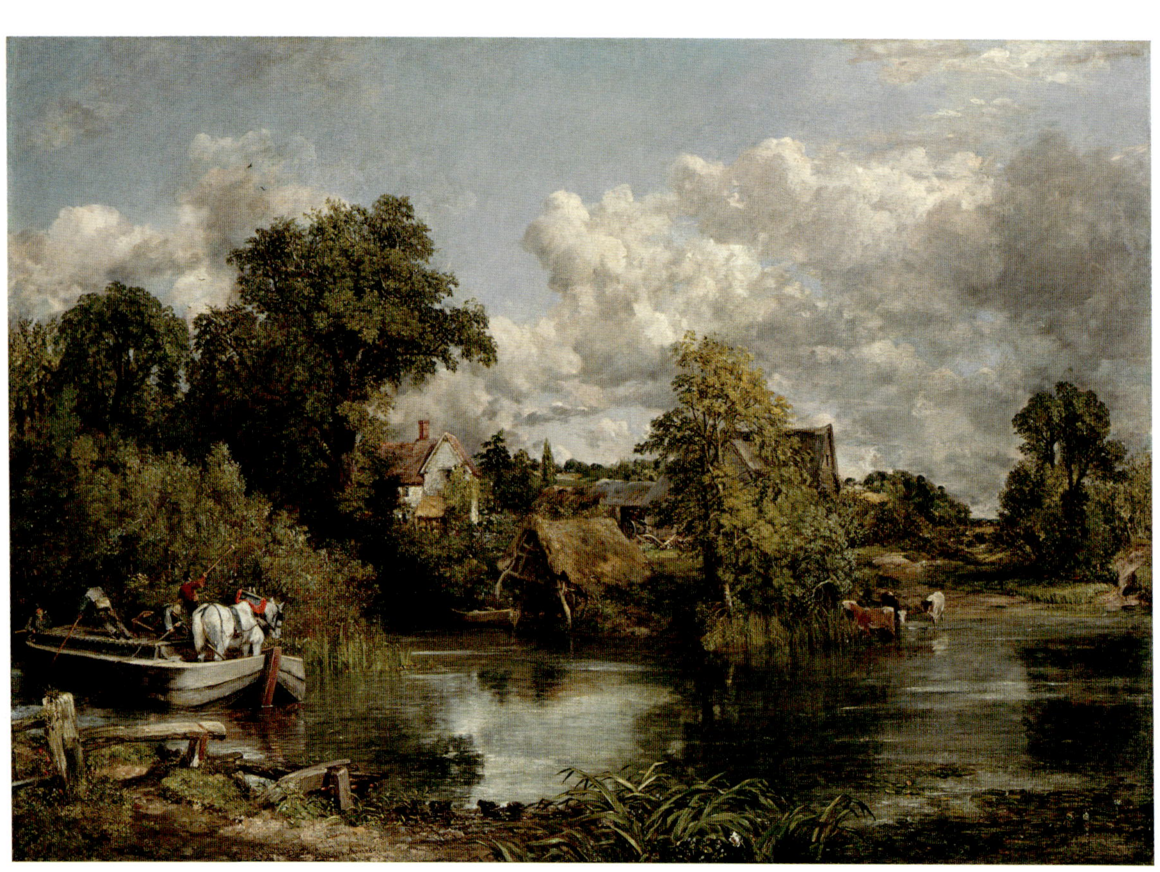

CONSTABLE'S WHITE HORSE

William Kentridge
Aimee Ng

The Frick Collection, New York
in association with D Giles Limited

g

FRICK DIPTYCH SERIES

Designed to foster critical engagement and interest specialist and non-specialist alike, each book in this series illuminates a single work in the Frick's rich collection with an essay by a Frick curator paired with a contribution from a contemporary artist or writer.

First published in 2020 by The Frick Collection
1 East 70th Street
New York, NY 10021
www.frick.org

Michaelyn Mitchell, Editor in Chief
Christopher Snow Hopkins, Assistant Editor

In association with GILES
An imprint of D Giles Limited
66 High Street
Lewes, BN7 1XG, UK
gilesltd.com

Copyedited and proofread by Sarah Kane
Designed by Caroline and Roger Hillier,
The Old Chapel Graphic Design

Typeset in Garamond
Produced by GILES
Printed and bound in Italy

Cover and pages 8, 10, and 24: details of John Constable, *The White Horse*, exh. 1819
Frontispiece: John Constable, *The White Horse*, exh. 1819. Oil on canvas, 51¾ × 74⅛ in. (131.4 × 188.3 cm). The Frick Collection, New York; Purchased by The Frick Collection, 1943 (1943.1.147)
Page 6: *The White Horse* in the Frick's West Gallery

Note to the Reader: For Constable's paintings first exhibited at the Royal Academy of Arts, the date is given "exh. [year]," with the assumption that the painting was made in or around that year.

A CIP catalogue record for this book is available from the Library of Congress.

ISBN: 978-1-911282-70-9

CONTENTS

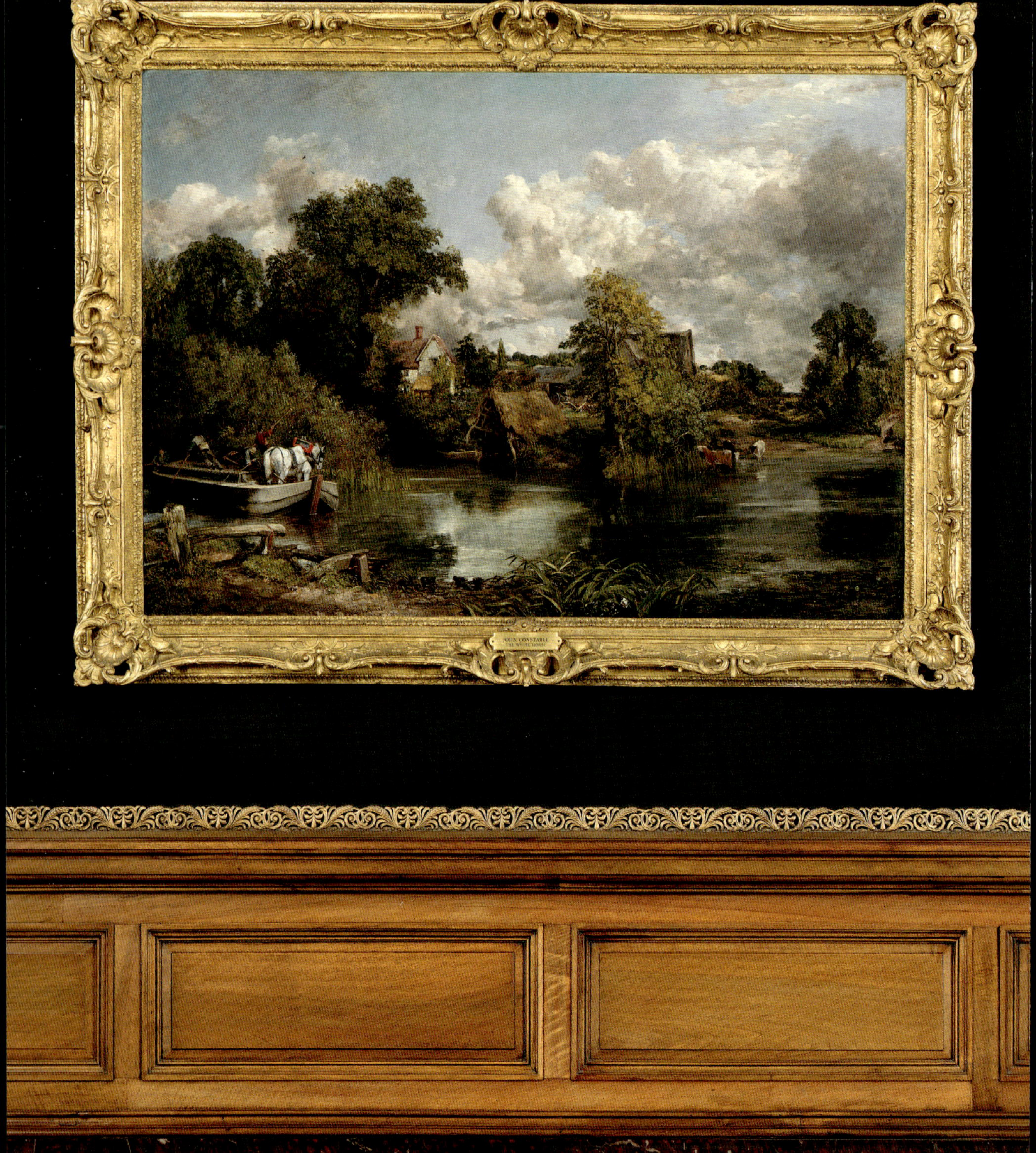

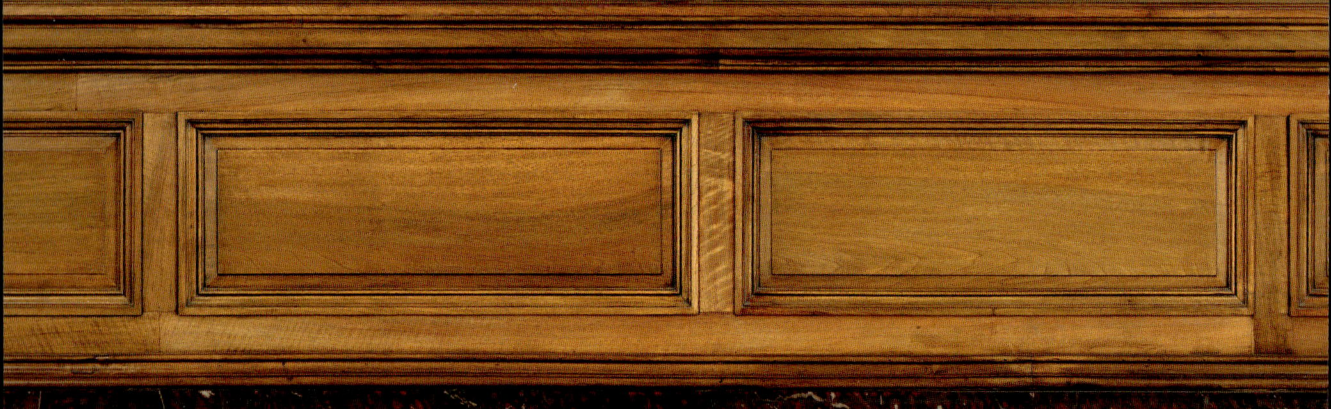
JOHN CONSTABLE

DIRECTOR'S FOREWORD

One of the first Romantic artists to elevate the English countryside to a subject for high art, Constable celebrated everyday rural life in monumental paintings like the Frick's *White Horse*. Recognition was slow in coming in his native land, but in France he was praised by artists like Eugène Delacroix and Théodore Géricault, as well as by a younger generation of French painters. For the naturalism of his depictions of nature and rural life, Stendhal admired Constable's works as a "mirror of nature."

In this fifth book in the Frick's Diptych series—and the first with a landscape as its subject—Frick Curator Aimee Ng deftly discourses on what Constable described as one of his "happiest efforts," and the artist William Kentridge evocatively writes about *The White Horse* from the perspective of the contrast between the world represented in the painting and memories of his childhood. Our immense thanks go to them both for these complementary texts.

Others to whom gratitude is extended include Xavier F. Salomon, the Frick's Peter Jay Sharp Chief Curator; Gemma McElroy, Curatorial Assistant; and Editor in Chief Michaelyn Mitchell, who managed the production of the publication and, with Assistant Editor Christopher Snow Hopkins, edited the texts. We would also like to acknowledge our longtime publishing partner, D Giles Limited.

Ian Wardropper
Anna-Maria and Stephen Kellen Director, The Frick Collection

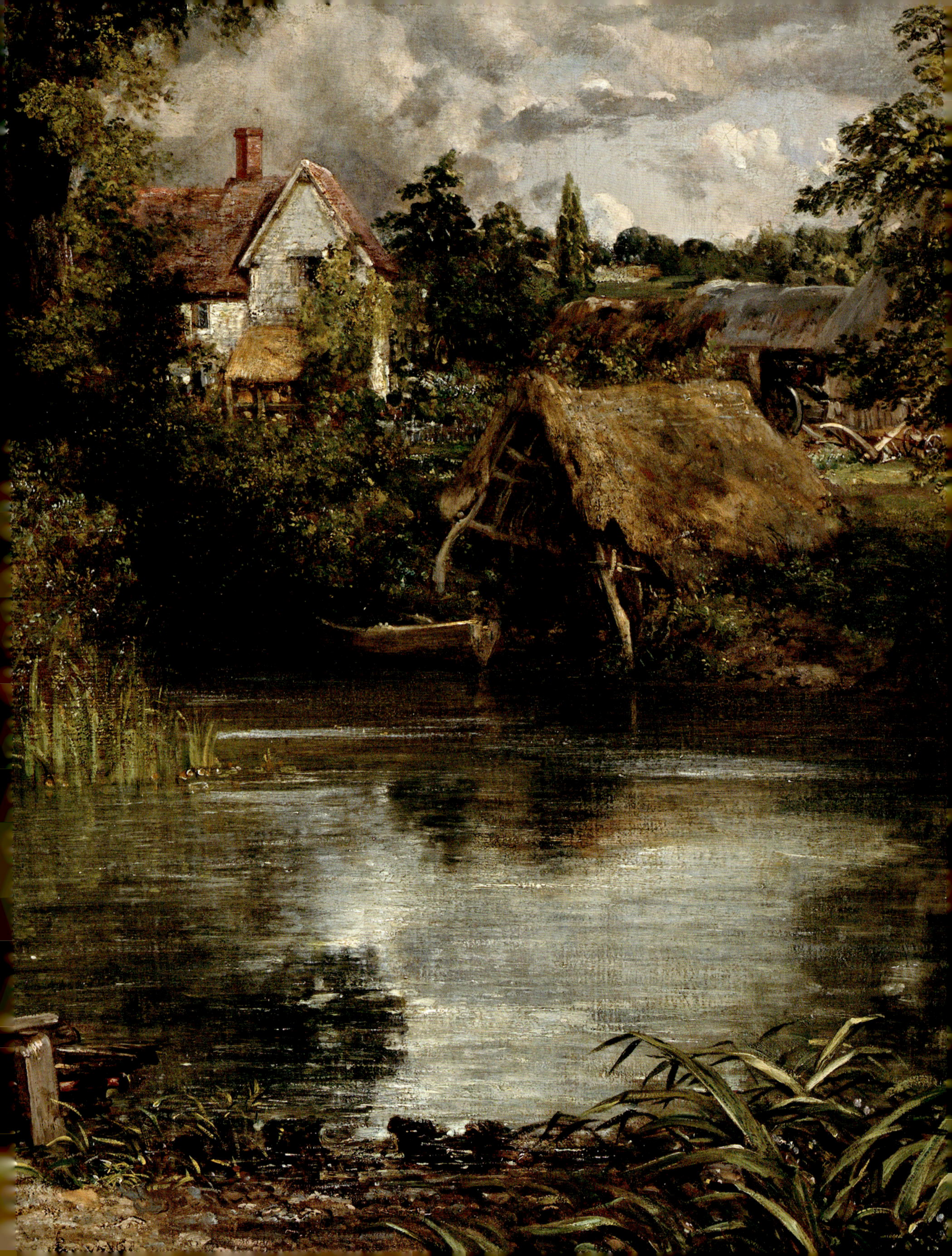

ACKNOWLEDGMENTS

For their generous help with this project, I wish to thank Nancy Anderson, Jessica David, Patrick Elliott, Mark Evans, David Franklin, Michael Gallagher, Meredith Gamer, George Goldner, Sandra and Andrew Graham, Catherine Hess, Franklin Kelly, Anne Lyles, Melinda McCurdy, Zara Moran, Evan Read, Jennifer Tonkovich, and Francesca Whitlum-Cooper. I thank esteemed conservators Sarah Cove, founder of the Constable Research Project, and Charlotte Hale, Conservator at the Metropolitan Museum of Art, for their help in investigating and interpreting technical aspects of Constable's painting. I am deeply indebted to Tim Barringer, Paul Mellon Professor of the History of Art at Yale, whose generous and incisive comments on my text improved it enormously; any errors are of course my own.

At the Frick, thanks go to Carolyn Thomas and my colleagues in the Archives Department, especially Susan Chore, as well as Patrick King and George Koelle. Xavier F. Salomon offered essential suggestions for the essay, for which I am very grateful. I thank Editor in Chief Michaelyn Mitchell for her patience, encouragement, and expert editing; she was aided by Assistant Editor Christopher Snow Hopkins. Very little of what I do at the Frick can be accomplished without the support and talent of Curatorial Assistant Gemma McElroy, to whom I owe the greatest thanks and highest praise.

It was a privilege to spend time with William Kentridge and *The White Horse* in the Frick's West Gallery. Reading his words and hearing him speak about the painting were both riveting and humbling, and I hope our texts in this volume can continue our conversation.

My husband, Simon Lewis, all too often must play the barge-horse of our family. With gratitude for his strength, tolerance, and caring counsel, I dedicate this book to him.

Aimee Ng
Curator, The Frick Collection

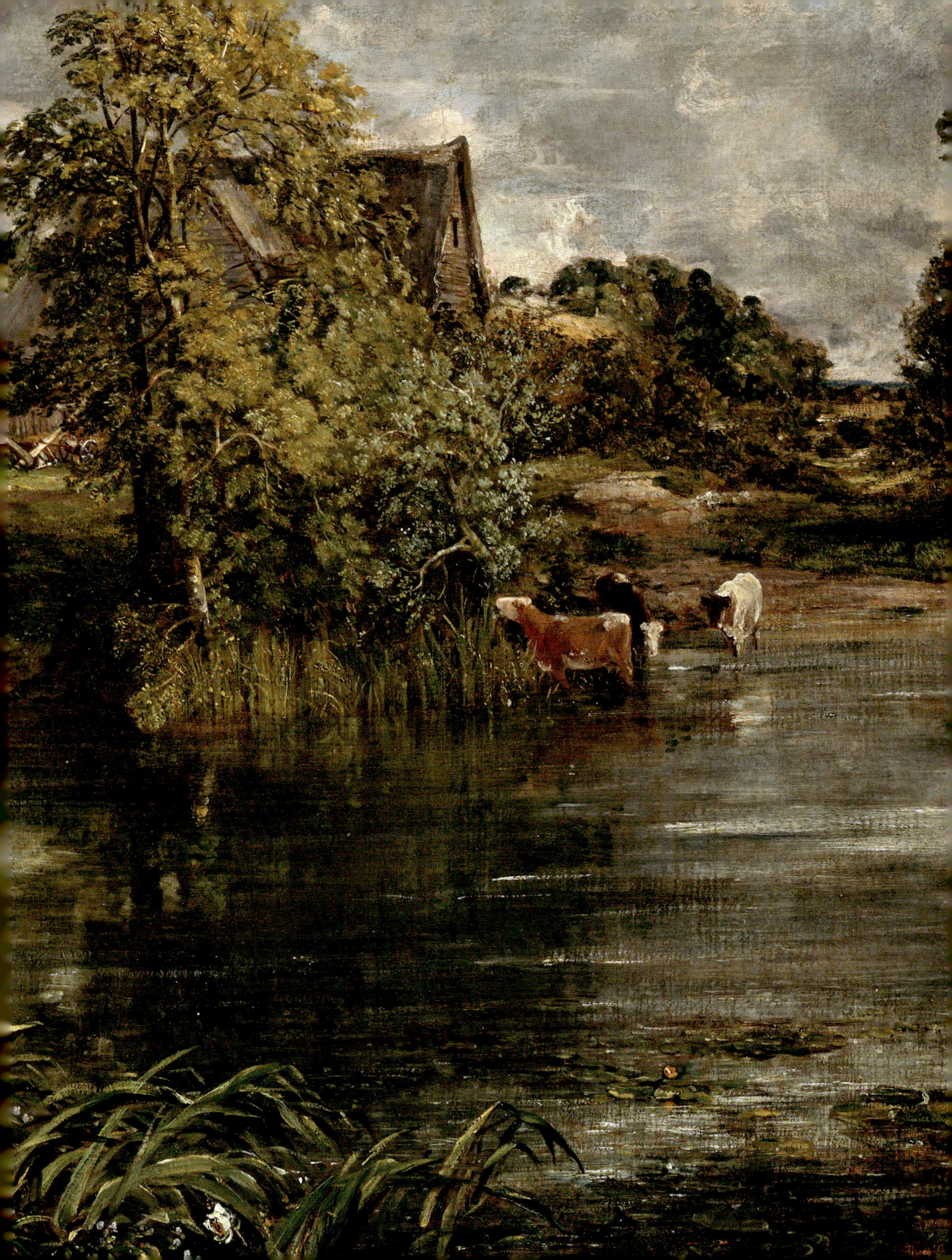

FINDING THE DAPPLE

William Kentridge

The Problem of Green

I remember my sister's eleventh birthday. We piled into the Austin A95, and my father drove the family—my father, my mother, my sister, me—out of the city, past the mine dumps, the warehouses, and the factories that ring the south of the city, through the plots and smallholdings, to the edge of the countryside. In Johannesburg, the leafy suburbs correspond to the end of irrigation and white privilege. The millions of trees planted in the earlier twentieth century make the northern suburbs a rich forest (of mostly exotic trees, pin oaks, elms, plane trees). Left to themselves, the koppies, or small hills, and ridges of Johannesburg would be parched and scrubby, the wild grass a dry white in winter, the trees a dusty olive gray. Driving out of the city, we'd left the shade and the green. Barbed-wire fences rather than stone walls or hedges of the suburban divisions. The plastic bags caught in the barbed wire were the wild flowers of the English riverbanks. We were in a landscape defined as much by engineering as by geological formation. There were lines of pipes, power lines, firebreaks burnt in the veld. You need a ruler or a steady hand to depict much of the countryside around Johannesburg.

A small oasis of green, a thin river, reeds and willow trees, a rowing boat, and a box of cherries. What was the pleasure? Certainly the safe domesticity of the boat; the surprise of my mother joining us at seeing who could spit the cherry stones the farthest into the water, my father with his rolled-up trouser cuffs and shirt sleeves, handling the oar so masterfully (so it seemed to my nine-year-old self); the dappled light, the movement of the reeds, the wind in the trees. Even now, fifty-four years later, there is a perfection in the memory, and I pause, caught in a double memory. The wind in the trees was also *The Wind in the Willows*. Here we were, just messing about in a boat. My father was Badger, and, while the rest of us were not Ratty or Mole, we were deep in that English idyll (the place of the picnic was even Henley-on-Klip).[1]

I find it impossible to separate the somatic pleasure of the shade, the amniotic comfort of the water, the richness of the greens in the trees, the darker green reflected in the water—to separate this immediate pleasure from the secondary one of the imagined home this felt like, the terrain filled with how it was meant to be, a view of land learned rather than found. How much of the pleasure was innate, a relief from the dryness found in the shadows, a relief from the blinding brightness of the sun, the green itself a relief to the cones and rods of the eyes? And how much of this immediately felt relief was constructed?

Where did this English idyll come from? From children's books—from the illustrations in these books, from the greens of the paintings or reproductions of paintings, of a world drowning in green. *The Wind in the Willows* stands in for so many others that have, as their premise, a rural Englishness. The *William* books by Richmal Crompton, with their English village life, the barn, the brook, the vicarage, the field hedgerows, the outlaws, and William. How could I avoid some connection to William? If my name had been Chaim (my Hebrew name), would I have had a different sensibility? The surname Kentridge is complicit in this. (My great-grandfather, a cantor in the synagogue, changed the name from Kantorovich in 1908 to this invented English-sounding name.)

In winter, when we have no rain for four or five months, all remaining color is leached from the land, a mixture of the dryness and the glare of the unremitting sun. So the spring green and the wetness of the birthday picnic were a blessing.

To Unlearn Taste (If We Could)

The training of sensibility went beyond childhood books, though this is still so strong. What was provoked was a longing for a world different from my own, a disappointment at being at the edge of a promised land, even as it became clear that this promised land was itself illusory. I wanted the world to be as depicted in these books. I spoke English, I could understand the jokes, the wordplay in the books. How could it not be my world?

Secondhand Green

Let me say it again—I love the greens in the Constable painting. But I feel I should be able to hold a distance from this seduction. I avoid these greens in my own work, but that is due to a cack-handedness in mixing colors rather than any stoic refusal of color. The beautiful unopened tubes of Winsor & Newton paints promised all the colors one could want, but, when I started to mix colors, the greens would be too heavily bright or turn into an olive ochre. I cannot hold a tune. When I sing, I hear the song in my head, but what comes out of my mouth is so far off, not just sharp or slightly flat but off by several tones. The same tone deafness dogs my attempts at mixing color. I would be glad to think that this might stem from a deep suspicion of oil paint and its universalizing tradition, but incompetence is a more accurate description.

There was a happy meeting of charcoal with the terrain outside Johannesburg when I started drawing it. There was no decision or principle involved. Charcoal was the medium I had been using for several years. And the landscape is a charcoal drawing itself, black stubs of grass after the winter fires. Drag a sheet of paper or a canvas behind a tractor, and the landscape draws itself (I did try this once, but the drawing was a dull gray; the burnt stalks of grass look like charcoal but do not have the richness of carbon needed for the blackness one hopes for).

Wanting and Not Wanting

Every week, my mother would return from the CNA[2] with my sister's and my comics. They were three months out of date. These were English comics: *Hotspur*, *Princess*, *Tiger*. This was an era of great illustration and draftsmanship. In the way that I now look at a hand drawn by Rembrandt and wonder how he could render it so full of old age and softness and folds and with so few etching marks, I used to marvel at how perfectly a soccer ball could be drawn curling into the net, or the perfect balance of a schoolboy batsman following through on his off-drive (the boy who was chained to his bat, a favorite of my father's too[3]). I still love this draftsmanship, the double seeing it implies. The action, the figure (the goalkeeper at full stretch pulling off another unbelievable save to win the game), and the line used to make this. How did the illustrator know how the leg changed at the knee? How did he know how to draw the hand flexed at the wrist? There is a triple seeing—the line, the figure, and the movements before and after the moment fixed in the drawing.

The movement from what we see on the paper and the flowering of an image in the brain still astonish me. You don't just see the final image, you see the complete cricket stroke, the complete leap of the goalkeeper.

This multiple seeing is, of course, at work in painting too. Here *The White Horse* stands in for so many paintings, not only landscapes. The flecks of paint being both brushmarks and leaves; the snowflakes of white touching the surface of the painting being a record of both the brush moving across the surface and the sunlight hitting the leaves, the lock, the water; the leaves made by dabs of paint over the sky or the sky made by dabs of paint over the green of the leaves. At the same time, paint on the surface and leaves and the sky behind the leaves.

The painting of water, learning the grammar not of water but of transforming the water into paint. At the art lessons I took as a child, I learned that vertical lines denote reflection in the water, that horizontal strokes breaking up the reflection make the surface of the water. The paint is always doubled, being itself and the world outside the canvas. These two layers were evident. Later, I would marvel at the *Tintin* books, not only for the draftsmanship but for their narrative skill, how from five frames on a page you would see a whole action sequence with anticipation, danger, action, and result. The marvelous pact of reading and recognition between artist and viewer.

But there was a fourth layer that was opaque to me. The longing for this world. I was six years old when I was taken to England for the first time. I remember the rightness of the countryside, of the rivers, of the canals, of the locks. This world shown in the comics, in the children's books, in the Constable painting. But I remember being shocked by the sight of two boys about my age who were smoking at the side of a canal. A double question. Where were their parents that they could smoke? How could there be poor people in this landscape? Poor people were Africans and lived in South Africa. Though it goes without saying, let it be said that the great gap between English books and a South African childhood was the absence of black in all that green. Of course not a fault of Constable, Richmal Crompton, or Gerard Manley Hopkins but still enlarging the schism between their imagined world and the world in which I lived.

Did it push Africans in Johannesburg into invisibility? I don't think so, but it certainly increased the gap between different elements in my life. It was an unresolved and unresolvable paradox to be of the world and simultaneously not of the world. For years, this felt like a glitch in the system, something to be repaired. Now it seems that this—and similar paradoxes or riddles without solution—is an inescapable part of how we are in the world. Any deep comfortable immersion in a tradition feels spurious. All traditions are active constructions. The more solid the appearance, the more desperate the construction.

The world became compartmentalized. There were of course overlaps—the warmth of my African nanny and the coziness of the English nursery had points of overlap. The different worlds lived side by side, an irresolvable paradox. The longing for the green—was that from a double exclusion, a childhood not in Constable country, and an awareness of Jewishness, of being outside the automatic assumptions of vicarage, church, christening in the books? No Jews, as far as I can remember, in *Hotspur* or *Beano*. Much later, Daniel Deronda and Benjamin Disraeli showed a possible Jewish Englishness, but by then I think I had found the South African landscape.

The Vanishing Point (and Historical Certainty)

My grandfather gave me *Great Landscape Paintings of the World*. Hobbema's *Avenue* was on the cover. Included in the sixteen or eighteen images in the book was not *The White Horse* but Constable's painting of Salisbury Cathedral, as well as paintings by Giorgione, Poussin, Claude Lorrain, and Courbet (whose greens seemed so much less varied than Constable's).

I think I was twelve when I was given the book. The images were a lexicon and a lesson in painting, in looking. Lessons of what an artist did. But there was also a lesson on how the world was constructed. A mixture of the landscape revealing itself, the folds upon folds of hills disappearing into the distance of Italian Renaissance painting, and the construction of this world by the artist. Often a tree or a branch, a fifth or a quarter of the way into the picture from one side, framing a view held by the tree. I think of Constable's *Salisbury Cathedral* here.

The book suggested there was a consensus of what the world was and how to see it within the tradition. In this case, it was a varied group of pictures and became, if not a tradition, certainly a canon by selection in the book. Each picture was given a particular status by being printed separately on glossy paper and glued onto its corresponding page.

When I opened the book in 2018, its 1965 glue had dried out, and the tipped-in reproductions fluttered out to an extended pile on the floor. These were the images that the word *landscape* forced through, a world that both had an order and could be ordered by the artist.

The horizon, and somewhere on its line, a vanishing point, where everything converged. Two diagonal, not parallel, lines provoke a vanishing point. We cannot resist the destination, codified from Alberti onward. The conventions of reducing deep space onto the flatness of canvas or paper, the pressure of the sky above and the activity on the ground below, pushing us to a destination.

The vanishing point was a point of compression: you, your two parents, your four grandparents, your eight great-grandparents, widening out onto the list of names in the foreground. Pushing back toward you and up above you, like the clouds in the sky, your children, their progeny, and an expanding list with the self at the central point of pressure, at the vanishing point. A point of pressure between all that has made you and all that is expected of you.

. . . etc.
great-great-grandchildren
great-grandchildren
grandchildren
children
self
2 parents
4 grandparents
8 great-grandparents
16 great-great-grandparents
. . . etc.

The lineage could also be depicted in other types of ancestry, from Giorgione to Poussin and Claude Lorrain, to Constable, to Courbet, the Barbizon group, the Impressionists, the Post-Impressionists, Cézanne, Matisse, Pollock up to the self and the expansion outward of work yet to be made. At any rate, a tightening down of the world to a single point, a blindness to other ways of thinking of the land and its image. The vanishing point had its logic and its certainty. *The Avenue*, the Hobbema painting on the cover of the book of great landscape paintings, was the clearest demonstration of the power of the *vluchtpunt*, or vanishing point. The destination of the road could not be avoided, as if we knew where we were going.

On my sister's birthday picnic, I do not remember any uncertainty over the route, but there were many other journeys to find a picnic spot—hoping for a tree and water, dogged by arguments in the front seat of the car, maps turned one way and another, refolded, the resistance of the paper to finding the original folds. Disputes over lists of instructions friends had given us to find the perfect spot. Disputes over which road we should take, which was the fifth gate, where we should turn off the road, which was the roadside farm stall marked on one of the lists. The certainty of the road disappeared: there were three-point turns, reverses, going one mile further on the same road before turning back.

Our journey was a series of loops, sharp angles, tire tracks left in the dust of the dirt roads. Not a series of chance marks in the sand but a record of doubt, of uncertainty as to where to find the landscape we wanted. The drips and swirls of Jackson Pollock rather than the certainty of the world of Poussin or Constable. Constable may have rejected the formal grammar of the landscape he was expected to paint, but there is a deep contentment in his place around the River Stour in his paintings. It is his terrain.

We in the car were always outside of our land, happy for a break in it whenever another, more familiar, leafy, wet, dappled world emerged for a few meters. A culvert of a stream, a flat rock, the almost shade from an acacia tree, or at least a concrete bench and table at the edge of a national road, to crack the boiled eggs, to untwist the wax paper with the pinch of salt and pepper, to open the tin of sardines and balance the thermos flask of orange cordial. The ground in my memory was always hard and stony; we would perch rather than sit. There was no grassy bank to fall asleep on (and wake to find a white rabbit). We were on the lookout for ants. The ubiquitous barbed-wire fences of South African farms corralled us.

Avoiding the Picturesque

When I started drawing the landscape outside Johannesburg some twenty-five years after the birthday picnic at the river, it was as a revenge on the landscape. It was an anger primarily at myself for not being able to step away from the landscape, both land and painting I loved. But also an anger against the dry, uninviting bleakness. I decided that however bland or dull that landscape was, I would match it. Of course, as soon as I started drawing it, I was held by all those features that I had so disliked: the pylons, the stunted trees, the lack of trees, rivers, and mountains.

The landscape met the drawing halfway. The blinding contrast of the winter light, all white paper or dark shadow, drained of color. The dried grass had the

William Kentridge
Remembering the Treason Trial, 2013
Lithograph in sixty-three panels, mounted on linen
76¾ × 70⅞ in. (195 × 180 cm)
Printed at The Artists' Press, White River, South Africa

blackness of charcoal; the lines of abandoned civil engineering projects were ready for rulers and a steady hand. This was in the mid-1980s, when the land around Johannesburg was becoming a post-industrial wilderness. The gold had been exhausted, mines were closed down, huge elements of cast iron and steel were abandoned in the veld. Roads were eaten away from their verges. But still these elements demanded the picturesque, as if the culvert were a river, the storm water drain a stone bridge, the poles of the wire fences another avenue of trees. I had to find a strategy to avoid this, to find a lack of structure or order in the terrain, to get the great landscape paintings out of my head.

I would choose a random distance—say 12.5 kilometers—drive that distance and then draw the landscape. But even then, I would frame the image in the most familiar way. Most of these drawings were made at the edge of the road, the vanishing point beckoning. To avoid even this seduction, I would find the image and then turn 180 degrees. I was half-successful. They were drawings I would not have arrived at in any other way, but there were many, in fact most of the drawings, that could not avoid my history of seeing. While the golden section was not directly evident, I was neither able nor willing to leave all to chance. And when I didn't leave all to chance, I couldn't escape the way my eyes had been constructed.

When I look at the Constable, I long for the certainty and confidence he had in his world. The workers on the field or on the river bank, a rational harmony that appears timeless. Even then, I knew the struggle he had to hold out against the demands made for the Italianate, for the Sublime, for the dramatic landscape. And his struggle—to make his portraits of trees as significant as the portraits of generals or dukes—was heroic.

Looking Backward

Constable's paintings of the area around the River Stour were already nostalgic. He was painting a memory of his childhood. *The White Horse* was painted in 1819. This was after the Napoleonic wars, when the drop in the corn price had brought about an economic depression. There was unrest in the country. This was the year of the Peterloo Massacre. There was widespread poverty; a whole new economic order was establishing itself. London's population tripled over Constable's working life.

Ninety thousand people applied to leave England, to immigrate as settlers to South Africa. Four thousand were chosen. Over a period of a few months in

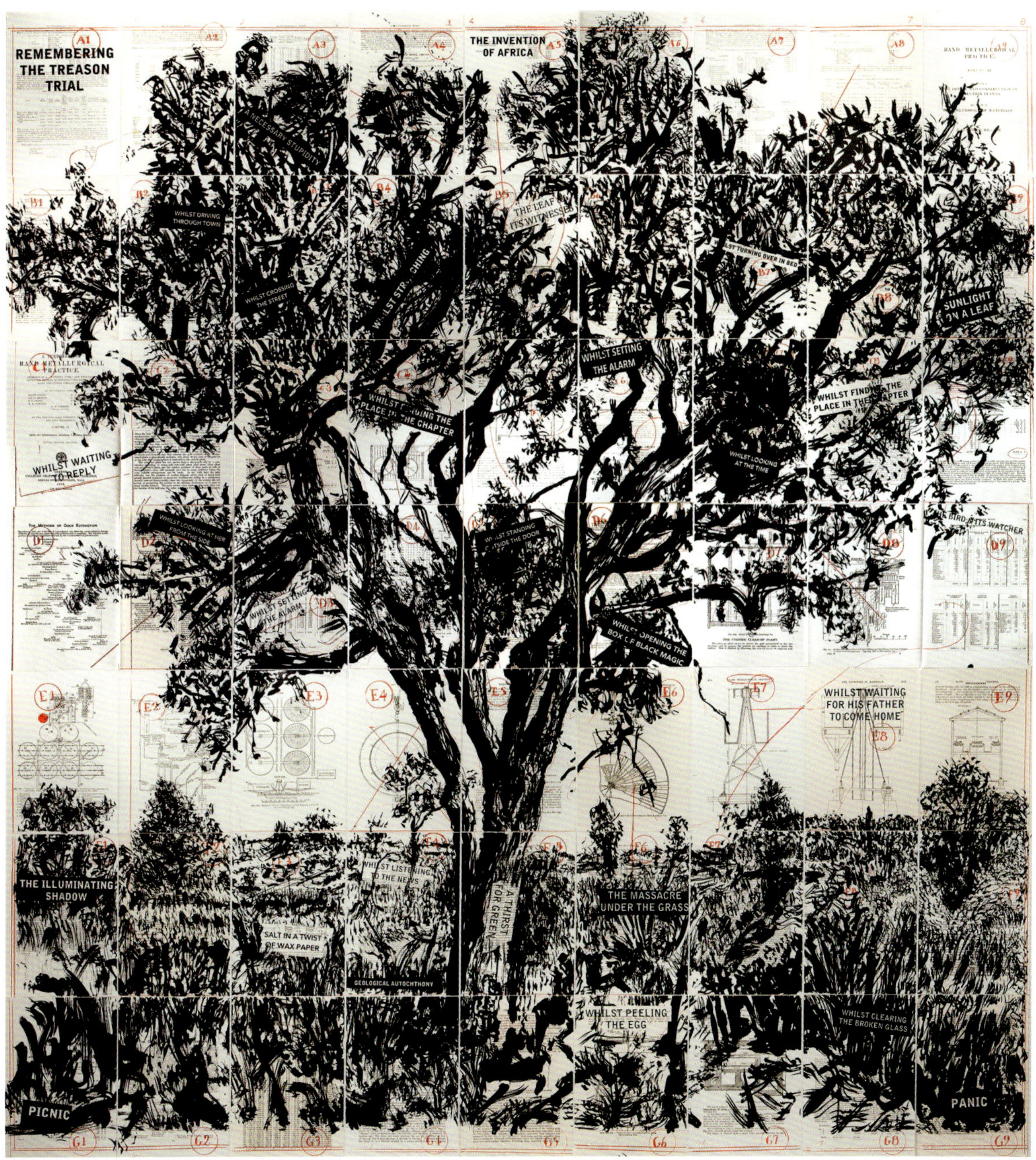
REMEMBERING THE TREASON TRIAL
THE INVENTION OF AFRICA
WHILST DRIVING THROUGH TOWN
WHILST CROSSING THE STREET
WHILST SETTING THE ALARM
WHILST LOOKING AT THE TIME
WHILST WAITING TO REPLY
WHILST WAITING FOR HIS FATHER TO COME HOME
THE ILLUMINATING SHADOW
WHILST LISTENING TO THE NEWS
A THIRST FOR GREEN
THE MASSACRE UNDER THE GRASS
SALT IN A TWIST OF WAX PAPER
GEOLOGICAL AUTOCHTHONY
WHILST PEELING THE EGG
WHILST CLEARING THE BROKEN GLASS
PICNIC
PANIC

1820, different parties of settlers arrived in South Africa and were given land at the eastern edge of the colony, a buffer against the indigenous inhabitants, the Xhosa, who were resisting the expansion of the colony. Earlier on in the Napoleonic wars, the British had taken over the Cape Colony from the Dutch, but, until the arrival of the 1820 settlers, Dutch had been the main European language spoken in the Cape. The settlers started the process of making South Africa aspire to an Englishness so that, even though my ancestors came from Lithuania and not England, English and its literature, rather than Yiddish, was what enfolded our house.

Constable, of course, was not a colonist, yet his view of England, his images, his colors, this view of England as "this other Eden, this demi-paradise, this little world"[4] were carried to South Africa as part of the colonial project. Certainly not carried by the settlers themselves—they had an understanding of England as a more Hobbesian world than Constable's, of each against each other, of life being brutish and short, where even the alien, inhospitable, dry Eastern Cape felt preferable to the world of desperation and poverty they were leaving in England. But the image of the idyll of England was carried by the descendants of these colonists; for the most part, this filled the air of what South Africa was in relation to England (for its white, privileged English-speaking population).

To read Constable in this light is unfair to him, but we can't avoid a reverse perspective, looking from the vanishing point backward, from Pollock to Matisse to the Impressionists, to the Barbizon school, to Constable—seeing how he was influenced by them and tracing the weight and pleasure of his paintings from suburban Johannesburg back to his studio.

The Horse of Course was a Baritone Too

In one of his *Proverbios*, Goya makes an etching of a horse balancing on a tightrope. The etching was made sometime between 1815 and 1823, during the same period that Constable painted *The White Horse*. Goya was also working in the aftermath of the calamitous peninsula war. His etchings for both *The Disasters of War* and the *Proverbios* show the inadequacy of conventional logic. He proposes a non-logic to show the limits of good logic.

Constable was working at the same time, and the traumas of the war were around him. But the war itself is almost invisible, its atrocities further away, and there are no such disturbances as one finds in Goya. Yet I cannot help seeing a similar absurdity in the horse on the boat. I know it is a report of a real circumstance; horses had to pull barges on the river, and, when the towpath changed from one side of the river to the other, horses would have to jump on board, be poled across the river, and leap off on the other side. But there is something of the indignity of a horse on a boat similar to the donkeys carried by men on their backs in Goya etchings and the tightrope-walking horse.

The two boatmen poling the boat with a horse have a similar theatricality. The angles of the bodies and poles take me back to the school for movement and mime I attended in Paris in the early 1980s, where we were taught the technique of pushing a boat with a pole as a piece of classical mime. The fifty-one movements of the boatman. Constable paints positions seventeen and thirty-one of these. The diagonals of the men and their poles show both natural action and the act of a commedia dell'arte artist.

Editing a Tree

But the horse and his attendants—the two men poling the barge, the man leaning over who is busy with the rope, and the old man at the rudder with his pipe—are bit players, almost off scene. The tall tree a third of the way in from the left acts as a second proscenium. The portraits of the trees and the foliage and the reflection in the water are the primary focus. The cows at the water's edge are extras in the drama.

How to paint this foliage? With what mark? How to paint this foliage in which a mark, no matter how fine, has to stand in for a mass of leaves? This is a studio problem, partly a question of seeing but more a question of transformation. How dry is the brush? Is it an opaque pigment or a series of glazes? Can the red-brown underpainting already make the leaves in shade? How much bright green needs to be flecked onto the edge of the tree to show the sunlight behind the tree lightening up just its edges? There is certainly a theatrical lighting in the painting. Some of the trees are in darkness, some fully in the spotlight. A convenient shadow on the distant trees allows the closer bushes to stand out. Constable is at once set designer, lighting designer, scriptwriter, and dramaturg in his painting. There is the grammar of the chosen material to learn and master.

When I started drawing the Johannesburg landscape, I could not find a mark for the leaves. A fine charcoal line could be a blade of grass, a strand of wire. A chamois leather cloth dipped in charcoal dust and wiped or dabbed or swirled on the paper made clouds. The material met the drawing halfway, but the multitude of short lines struggled to turn into leaves.

Sometime later, in the 2010s, twenty years after the first drawing of the Johannesburg landscape, I started drawing with Indian ink. I used Chinese calligraphic brushes; but as I did not know the correct care of brushes and was most probably using the wrong ink, the fine points of the brushes were lost and their tips became an unruly flaring of different clumps of hair. A single line descended into jagged, uncontrollable, almost parallel lines. Dabbed rather than brushed, the marks became an irregular splatter but with a controllable randomness. Through this uncontrollability, the bad brushes suggested the randomness of foliage. It could be made dense or less so by the lightness of touch, by the amount of ink, by the direction of the brush—straight, diagonal, or twirling—as it hit the paper.

The ink paintings were generally made on small pages, usually a dictionary. The tooth and absorbency of the paper is part of the grammar of making the image. And the tree would be grown from these pages. If the trunk is too short, add another sheet. If the leaves get too thick in one section, rearrange the sheets of paper. In one form or another, this is the usual practice of the studio, a construction rather than a description or recording.

Even the Constable landscape, which seems so immediate, is, the moment the barge crosses the river, a series of studio constructions. He is making a theater—set, actions, drama—all in one image. How we have to fight to resist the performance, to be both held by the painting and know that the image is provisional, a possible construction of the world. The world—that is to say the landscape, trees, river—is brought into the studio. There it meets so many visible and invisible partners, all waiting to be fragmented, rearranged, reconstructed, and sent back out into the world.

In the studio are the studies of clouds, fragments of trees, the pages of the leaves. Provisional sketches of final images. But also childhood memories of the River Stour, of the willow trees at Henley-on-Klip, the box of paints and the familiar palette knives, the Indian ink with the good brush and bad brush, the reports of the day, the memory of a Claude Lorrain painting, an old reproduction of *Salisbury Cathedral* pinned to the studio wall.

Notes

1 Kenneth Grahame's *Wind in the Willows*, published in 1908, is an Edwardian allegory of rural England, but it is not an entirely innocent book. People have read many things into it. The hidden homosexuality of Grahame and the genteel anti-Semitism in the character of *nouveau riche* Toad of Toad Hall represent the new order that tries to upset the tranquility of the riverine world of the water rat, the mole, the badger. This, of course, was invisible to me as a child and escaped the notice of my grandfather, who kept a close watch on English writers he deemed anti-Semitic. G. K. Chesterton and Father Brown were *personae non gratae.* This was the grandfather (my mother's father) who gave me the book *Great Landscapes of the World* and, a year later, one on Michelangelo's *Last Judgement.* I'm not sure how the Christ enthroned in the center of the image of the cover of the book passed muster. The illustrations to *The Wind in the Willows* by Arthur Rackham, such as the pollarded willow tree that has an older cousin in the tree in Constable's *Leaping Horse*, are a deep substratum of images that sit in my head, waiting to connect with images still arriving fifty-five years after I saw these illustrations.

2 The Central News Agency, a bookshop, stationery store, and receiving depot of magazines and comics shipped from England.

3 This comic strip, the ongoing story of a boy chained to his bat, ran in the comic *Hotspur* from issue 244 to issue 255, from June 20 to September 5, 1964, when I was nine years old. It depicts a boy wonder sportsman whose father kept his cricket bat chained to his wrist to make him the best cricketer in the world. The series ended with the boy beating the world record number of runs in a test match. Appropriately, this was for England (I presume against Australia). The colonies had to play their appropriate role in these dramas, and we were good students.

4 This is from Shakespeare's *Richard II*, but lines from other poems from childhood come to mind that solidify and crystallize the image of this idyll. Gerard Manley Hopkins: "My aspens dear, whose airy cages quelled, / quelled or quenched in leaves the leaping sun" or the "wind-wandering weed-winding bank." This versus the barbed-wire fences festooned with plastic bags. And also from Gerard Manley Hopkins: "This darksome burn, horseback brown, his rollrock highroad roaring down." Fifty years after learning them, these phrases stick like an earworm, coming back as soon as the stream is seen, wind in trees is heard, or water is seen cascading over rocks.

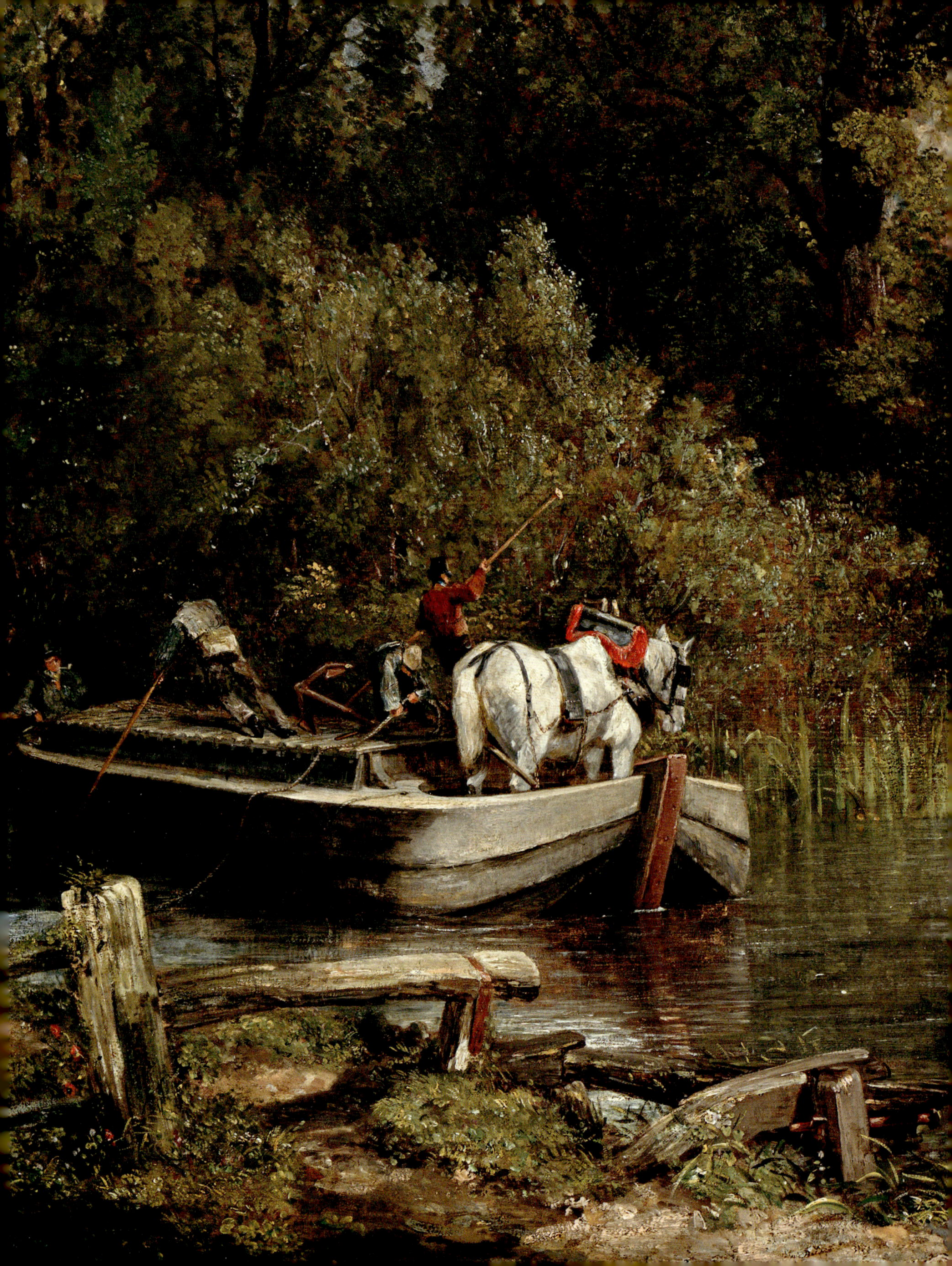

CONSTABLE'S WHITE HORSE

Aimee Ng

> There are generally in the life of an artist, perhaps one, two or three pictures, on which hang more than usual interest—this is mine.
>
> —John Constable to John Fisher, January 14, 1826

A towering figure in British art, John Constable has been credited with changing the course of European painting. Eugène Delacroix proclaimed him the father of French landscape painting, placing in his wake Romantic painters like Corot, Millet, and Rousseau. Consequently, it has also been suggested that the Impressionists were indebted to Constable, his art aligned with Cézanne's innovations and an influence on other French artists as diverse as Courbet, Manet, and Matisse. Lucian Freud, who saw something of Constable in Vincent van Gogh's *Boots*, chose his landscapes as the subject of a monographic exhibition he curated at Paris's Grand Palais at the turn of the twenty-first century. Constable has also been called, intriguingly, the "Jackson Pollock of the 1830s."[1]

Such associations would have horrified Constable, who had no interest in French art, and may bewilder some present-day viewers, especially because J. M. W. Turner, Constable's contemporary and rival, was a more obviously experimental painter. These differences were highlighted in the artists' submissions to the 1819 Royal Academy summer exhibition, with Turner's dramatic depiction of sailors attempting to retrieve overboard cargo in churning foreign waters (fig. 1) pitted against the pastoral tranquility of Constable's portrayal of a slow-moving barge on an English river in the artist's hometown (see fig. 3), a painting that has come to be known as *The White*

Fig. 1
J. M. W. Turner
Entrance of the Meuse: Orange-Merchant on the Bar, Going to Pieces; Brill Church bearing S. E. by S., Masensluys E. by S., exh. 1819
Oil on canvas
69 × 97 in. (175.3 × 246.4 cm)
Tate Britain, London; Accepted by the nation as part of the Turner Bequest 1856 (N00501)

Horse but which was then titled *Scene on the River Stour*.[2] But Constable's objectives were different from Turner's.[3] Two primary artistic goals occupied Constable. One was to gain recognition for what he termed "Natural Painture"—a practice, ostensibly rooted in science and direct observation, of imitating in paint as closely as possible effects of light and shadow, forms of clouds, and the appearance of dew, and of finding beauty in quotidian scenes. His cloud studies (fig. 2) have been prized as both scientific observations and artistic expressions. Naturalism distinguished Constable's landscapes; in them, one could "feel the wind blowing on [one's] face," as one viewer put it.[4] His other goal was to elevate what he called "English Landscape Scenery" as a respectable subject for high art, one that could rival portraiture and history painting. As he endeavored to attain the effect of "truth to nature" in local English subjects, an increasingly expressive, unfinished quality, with direct and unobscured brushstrokes, came to characterize his oil sketches and later paintings—hence the comparison to Pollock.[5] In his day, this quality was considered inappropriate for public exhibition.

Constable never left England, even refusing to travel to France to receive awards for his paintings, among them a gold medal given by the French king, Charles X.[6] England's countryside contained everything he wished to paint, and he believed himself to have been born to paint it.[7] Over the course of the twentieth century, Constable's landscapes became identified with England and with Englishness itself, representing the purity of a world as yet unspoiled by industrialization. But even as he painted them, most of his landscapes were somewhat nostalgic. His most famous recall his childhood in the area around East Bergholt, Suffolk, and along the River Stour. Born in the year America declared independence from Britain, Constable (1776–1837) lived through more than two decades of Revolutionary and Napoleonic wars (1793–1802, 1803–15). He was almost forty by the time injured soldiers returned from the British victory at Waterloo to unemployment in rural areas like Suffolk and general economic depression gripped agricultural communities across the country; his own family's businesses in mills and transport suffered for years after.[8] In a letter of 1822 to John Fisher, archdeacon of Berkshire (part of the diocese of Salisbury) and a close friend, Constable lamented how crime-ridden his home region had become.[9] None of this enters his paintings, however: he painted *The White Horse* nearly four years after Waterloo. With rare exception, Constable's art looked inward to his feelings and to his experience of places

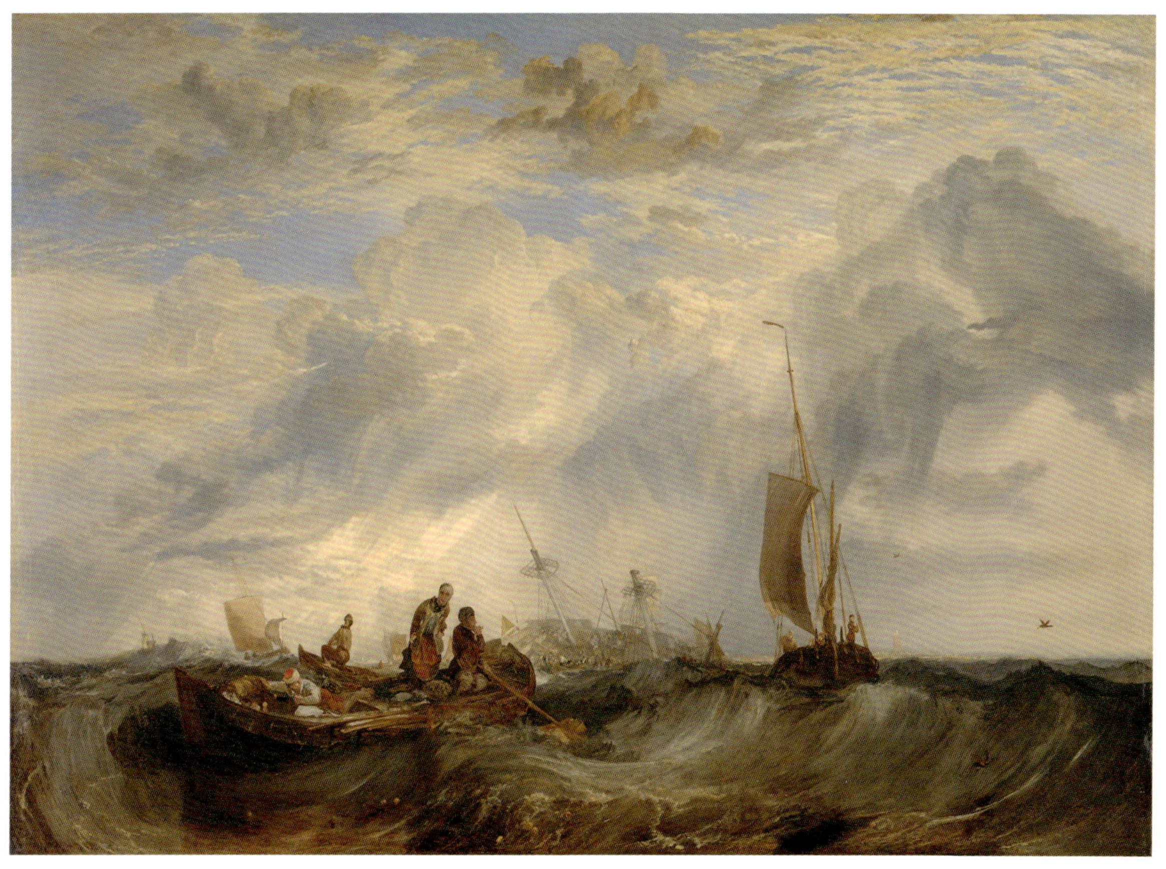

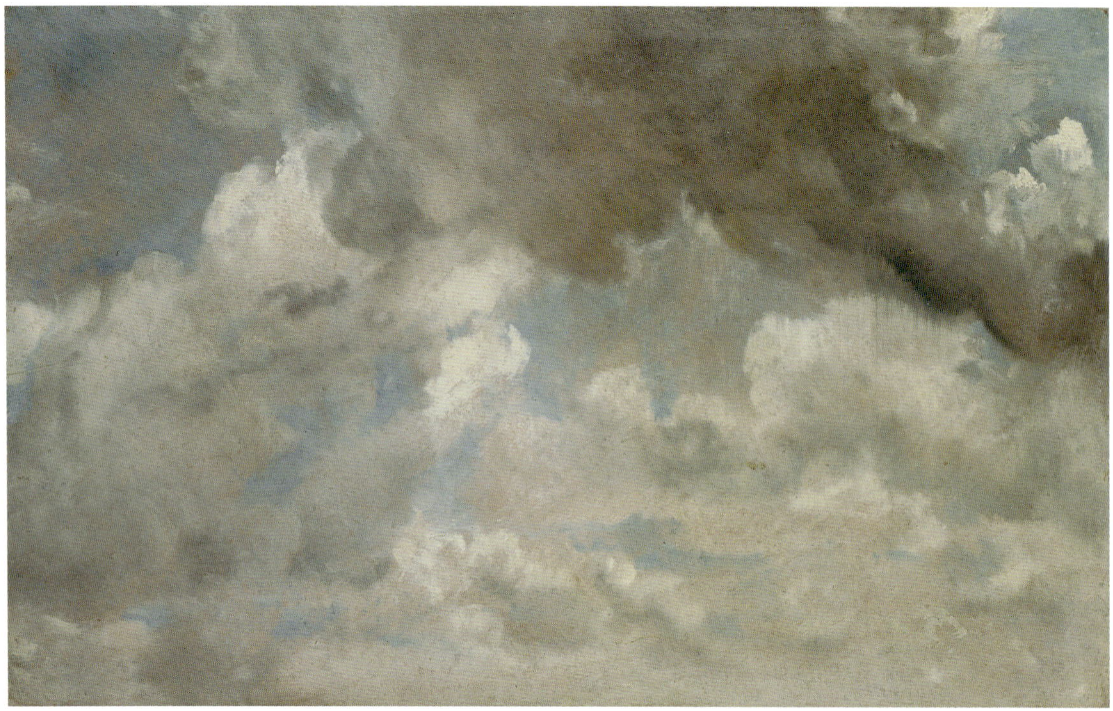

Fig. 2
John Constable
Cloud Studies, ca. 1822
Oil on paper, laid down on board,
each 11½ × 19 in. (29.2 × 48.3 cm)
The Frick Collection, New York;
Bequest of Henrietta E. S. Lockwood
in memory of her father and mother,
Ellery Sedgwick and Mabel Cabot Sedgwick,
2000 (2001.3.133, 2001.3.134)

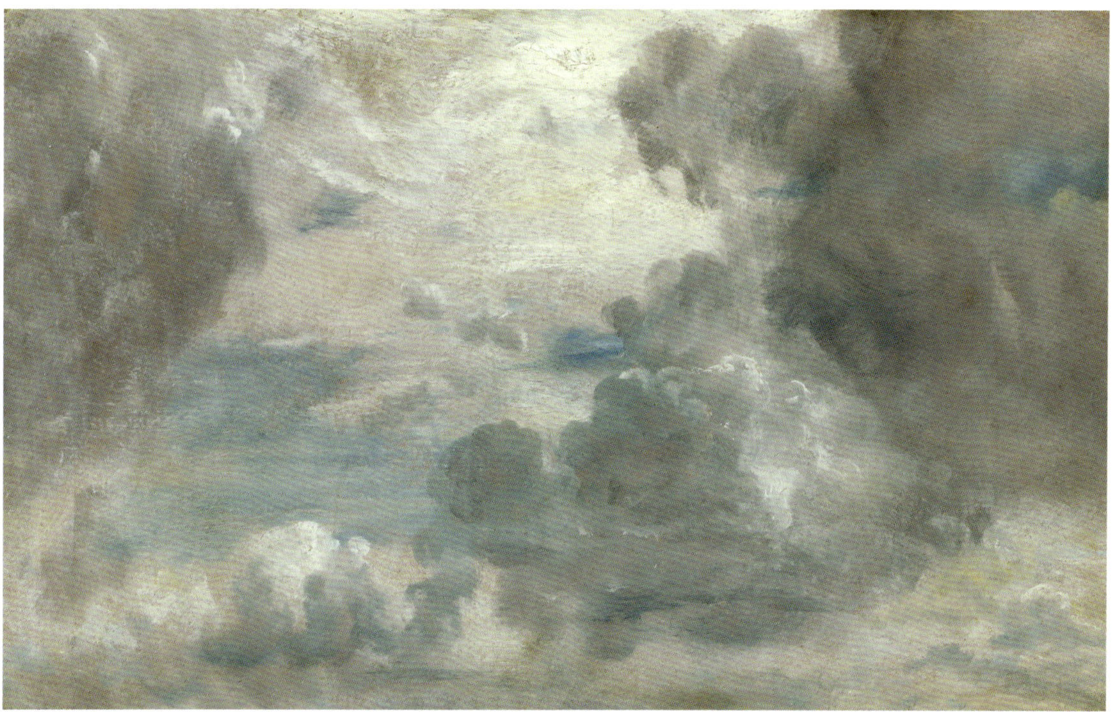

familiar to him. "I should paint my own places best," he wrote to Fisher. "Painting is but another word for feeling. I associate my 'careless boyhood' with all that lies on the banks of the Stour."[10] He offers highly naturalistic and personal depictions of the English countryside that no longer were—or perhaps never were—exactly as his paintings present them.

Constable painted a series of six monumental canvases that established him in the art world (figs. 3, 6, 7, 9–11). Known as the "six-footers," these paintings depict scenes along the Stour, and one of them, *The Hay Wain* (see fig. 7), has become a prized icon of English national identity.[11] *The White Horse*, however, is the first of these celebrated paintings, and its importance in Constable's career cannot be overstated. It was largely due to its favorable reception at the Royal Academy's 1819 summer exhibition that Constable was elected an associate member after nearly twenty years of effort. The painting was purchased by Fisher, who gave the painting its popular name.[12] In response to *The White Horse*, critics for the first time compared Constable favorably with Turner, who was more successful and better known, and with "Old Masters" like Ruysdael and Hobbema.[13]

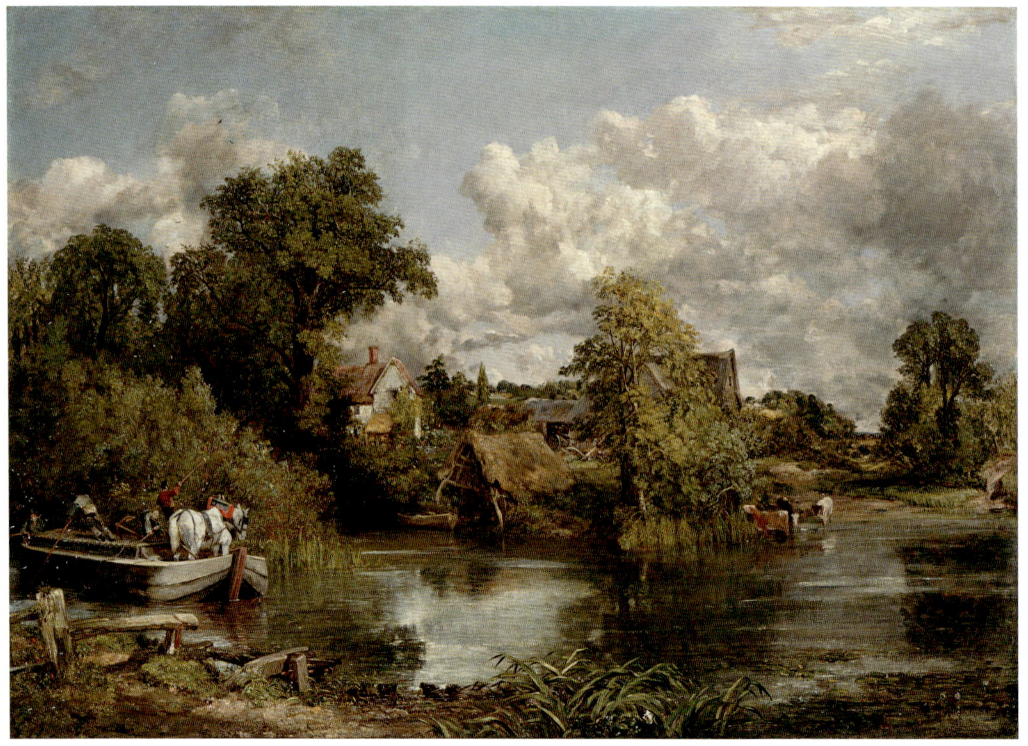

Fig. 3
John Constable
The White Horse, exh. 1819
Oil on canvas
51¾ × 74⅛ in.
(131.4 × 188.3 cm)
The Frick Collection, New York; Purchased by The Frick Collection, 1943 (1943.1.147)

Fig. 4
John Constable
The White Horse (full-size sketch), 1818–19
Oil on canvas
50 × 72 1/16 in. (127 × 183 cm)
National Gallery of Art, Washington; Widener Collection (1942.9.9)

Fig. 5
John Constable
The White Horse (full-size sketch, pre-treatment), 1818–19
Oil on canvas
50 × 72 1/16 in. (127 × 183 cm)
National Gallery of Art, Washington; Widener Collection (1942.9.9)

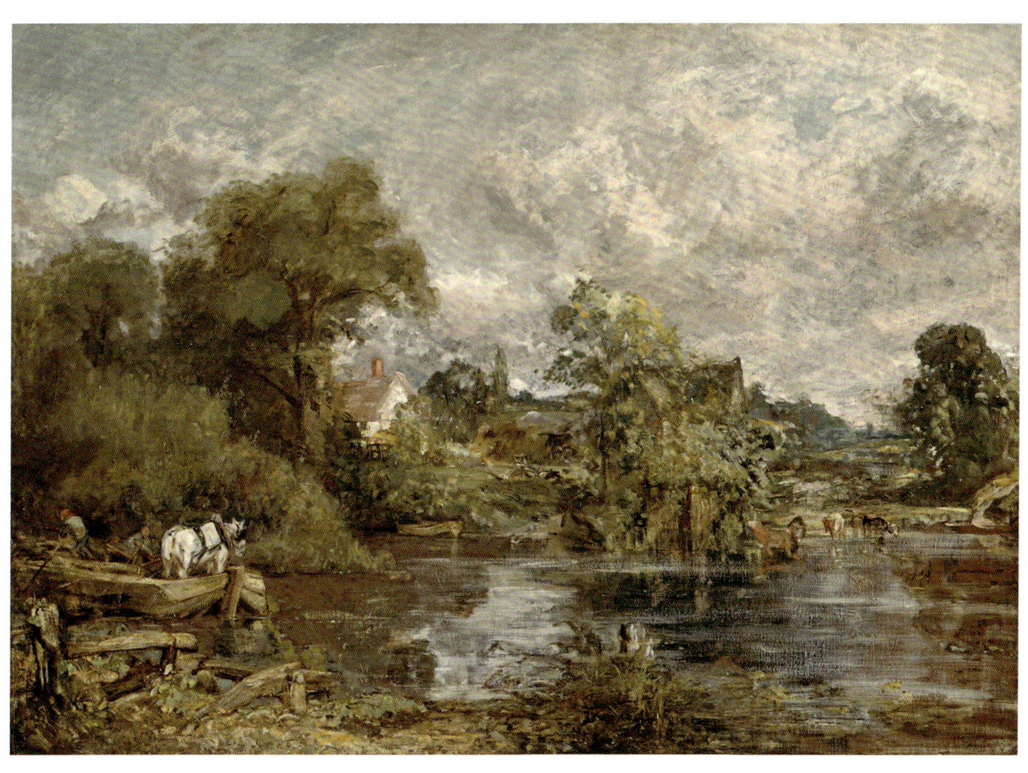

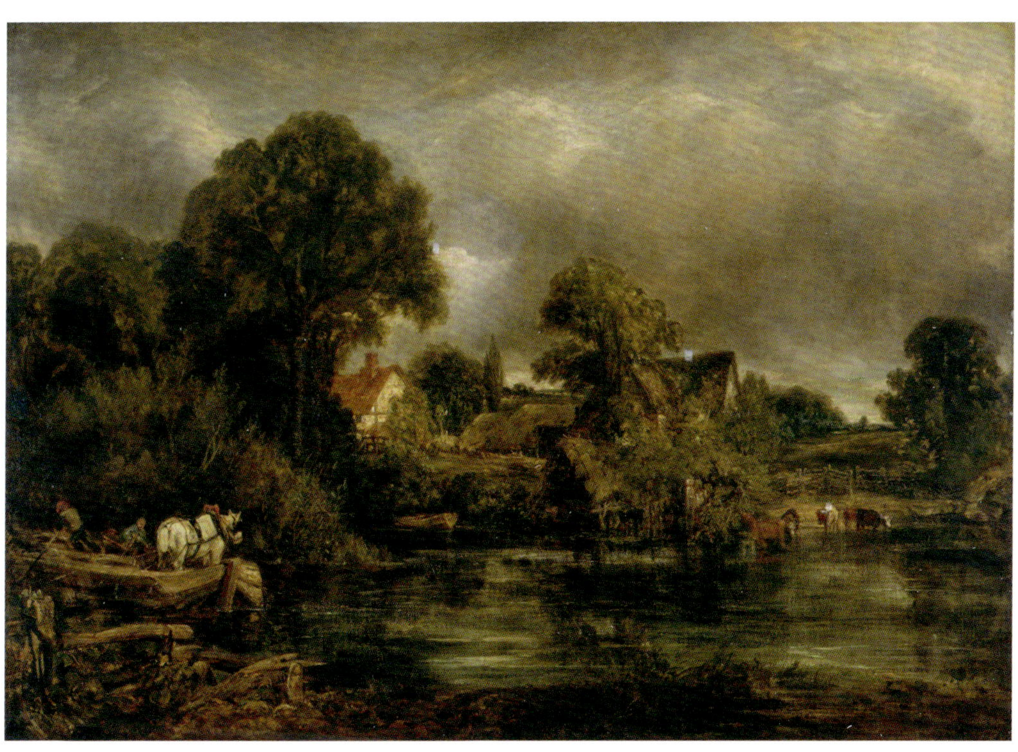

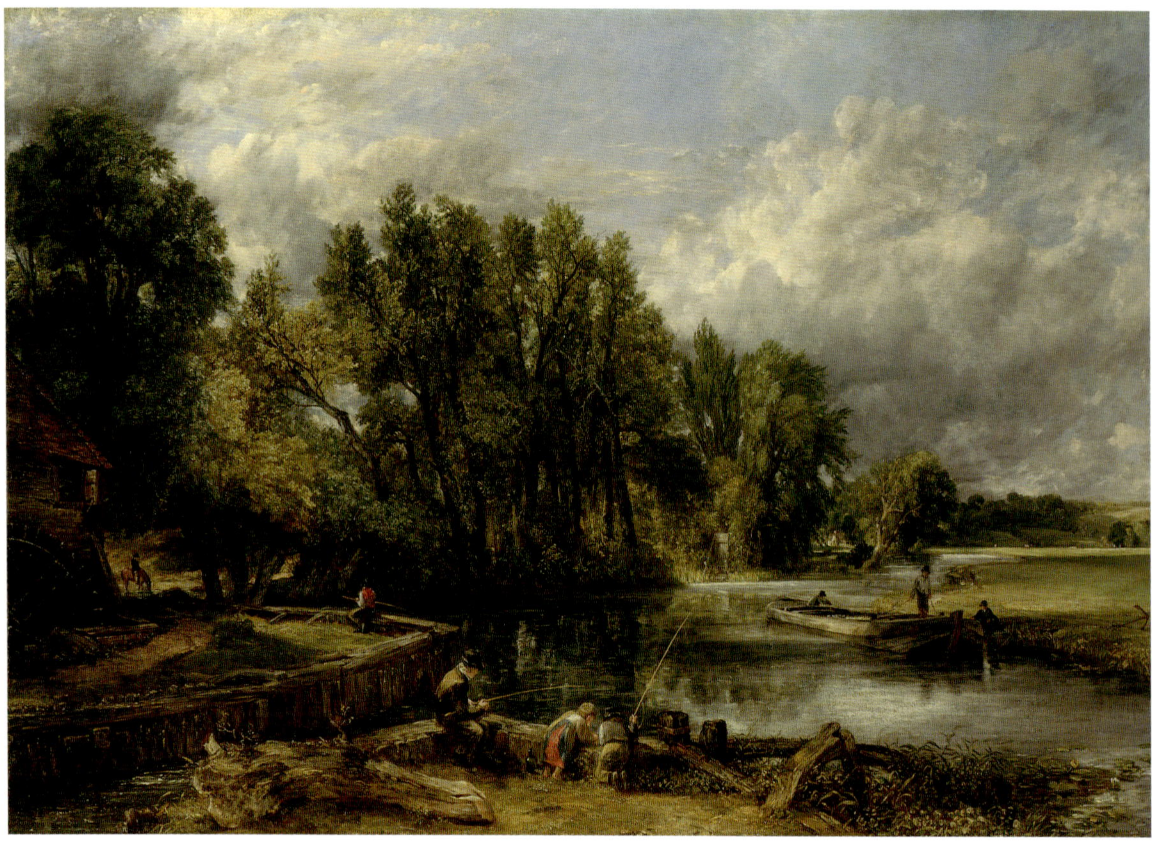

Fig. 6
John Constable
Stratford Mill, exh. 1820
Oil on canvas
50 × 72 in. (127 × 182.9 cm)
National Gallery, London;
Presented to the National Gallery under the acceptance-in-lieu procedure, 1987 (NG6510)

Constable described *The White Horse* as one of his "happiest efforts."[14] He exhibited it publicly three times: in 1819 at the Royal Academy and in 1825 first at the British Institution and then at the Salon in Lille, where the city awarded it a gold medal.[15] To some degree, his decision to send it abroad for exhibition had to do with its belonging to a friend willing to part with it for months at a time for the advancement of Constable's career. Not all of his clients were so generous. For example, John Pern Tinney, the owner of *Stratford Mill* (fig. 6), reluctantly sent it to the 1824 Paris Salon and refused to send it abroad thereafter. When it went to Paris, Fisher lent Tinney *The White Horse* to hang in its place in his home.[16] Beginning in 1830, Constable had full control over *The White Horse*, for in this year Fisher had to liquidate assets, and Constable bought it back from him at the original purchase price of one hundred guineas.[17] The painting remained in the artist's possession until his death in 1837; at the sale of his studio one

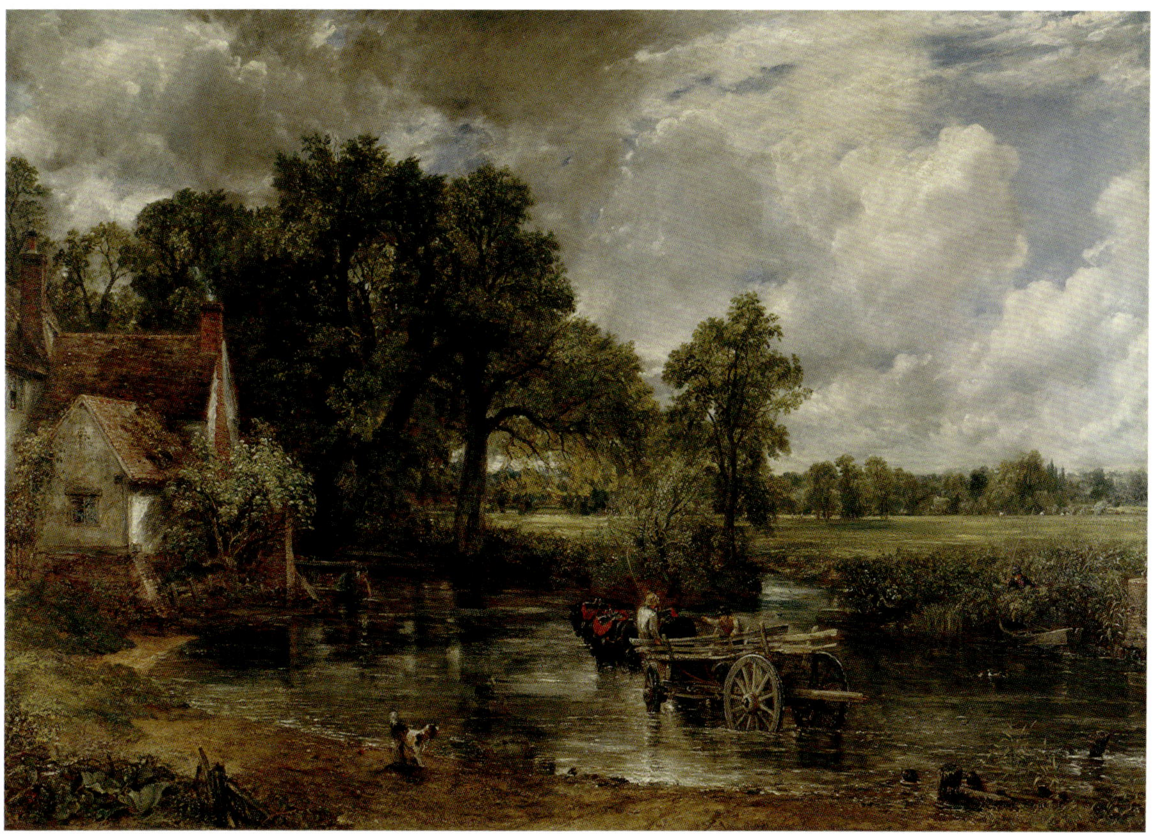

Fig. 7
John Constable
The Hay Wain, exh. 1821
Oil on canvas
51¼ × 73 in. (130.2 × 185.4 cm)
National Gallery, London;
Presented by Henry Vaughan,
1886 (NG1207)

year later, it fetched one hundred and fifty guineas, the highest price of all the lots sold.[18]

At the time of its presentation in 1819, *The White Horse* was the largest landscape he had exhibited; this was in part a tactic to draw attention to his art through sheer size.[19] The Academy's exhibitions at Somerset House were crowded with hundreds of works, jostling for attention: to paint on a grand scale was one way to ensure that the public took notice. For the first time, he produced a preliminary full-size oil sketch (see fig. 4), a costly and time-consuming practice that he would repeat for the five subsequent River Stour six-footers and other works.[20] With no precedent in European art for the systematic production of full-size oil sketches on canvas for monumental paintings, Constable invented an approach to developing compositions that essentially entailed painting two versions of the same size for each work. The practice evolved over his career, with his "exhibition" paintings (those

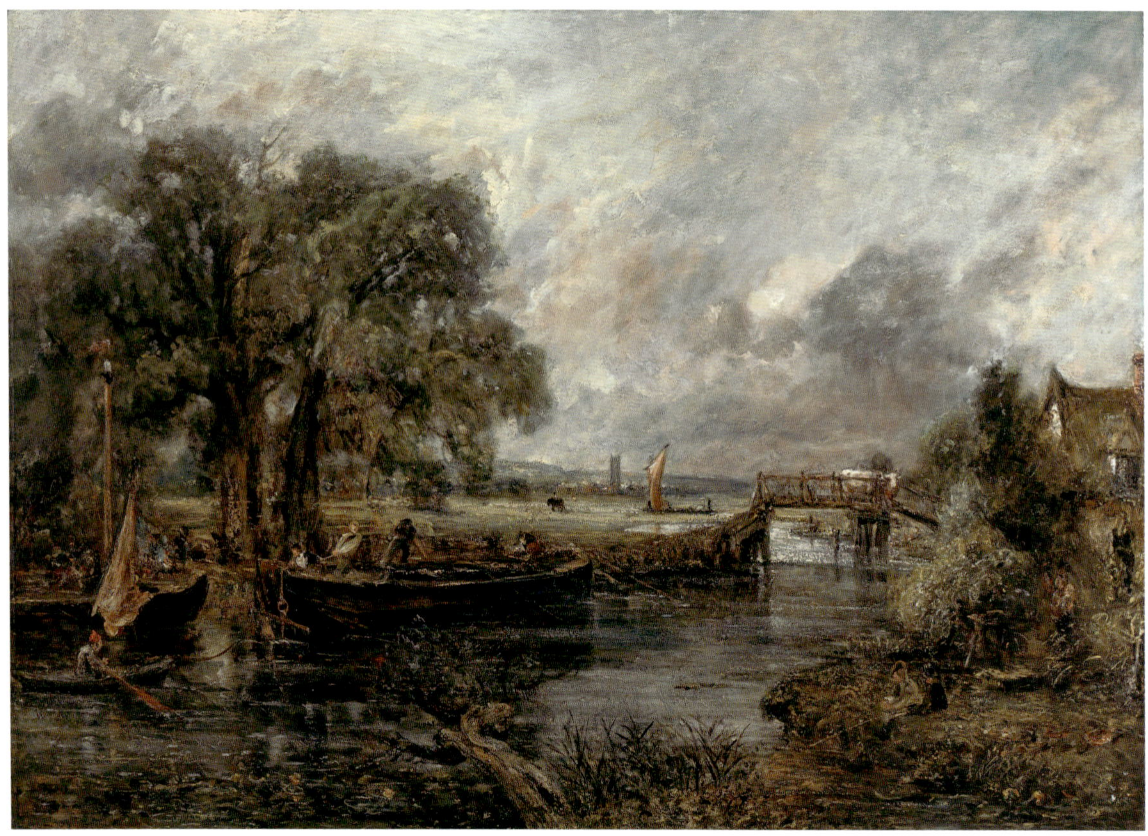

Fig. 8
John Constable
View on the Stour near Dedham
(full-size sketch), ca. 1821–22
Oil on canvas
51 × 73 in. (129.4 × 185.3 cm)
Private collection

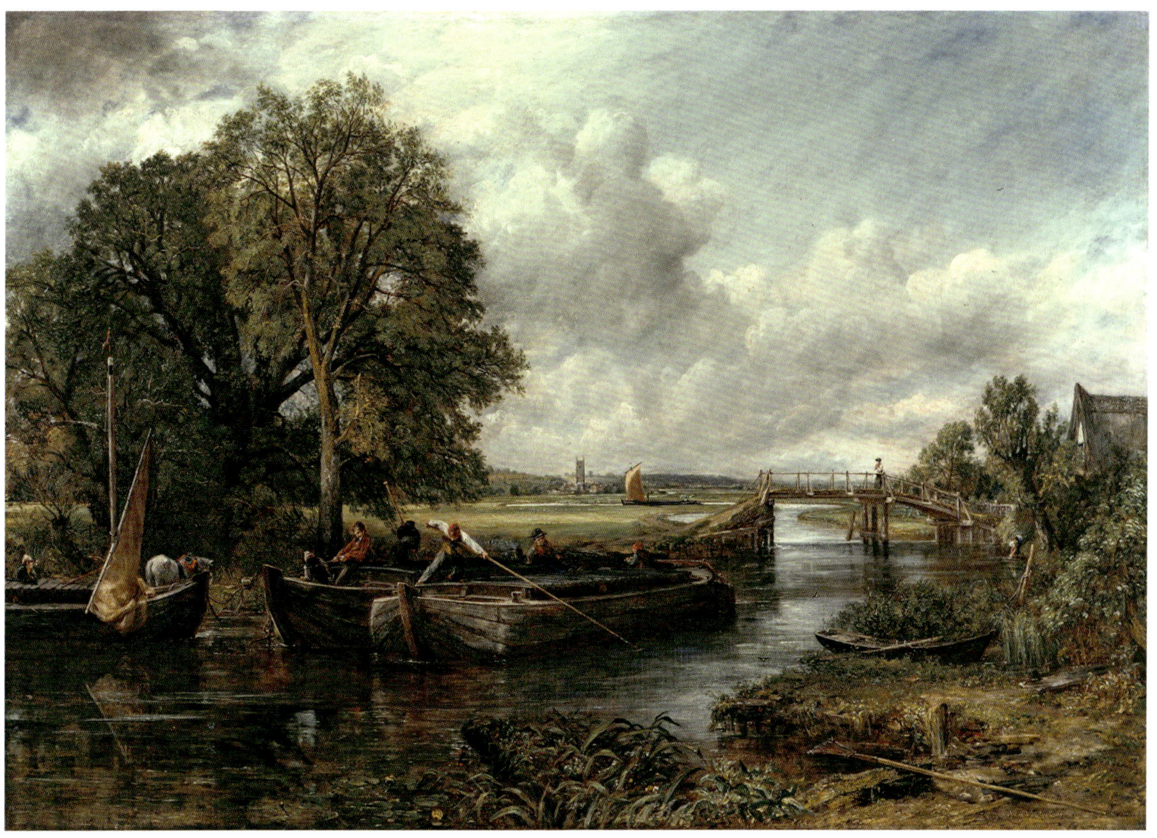

Fig. 9
John Constable
View on the Stour near Dedham,
exh. 1822
Oil on canvas
51 × 74 in. (129.5 × 188 cm)
The Huntington Library, Art
Museum, and Botanical Gardens,
San Marino (25.18)

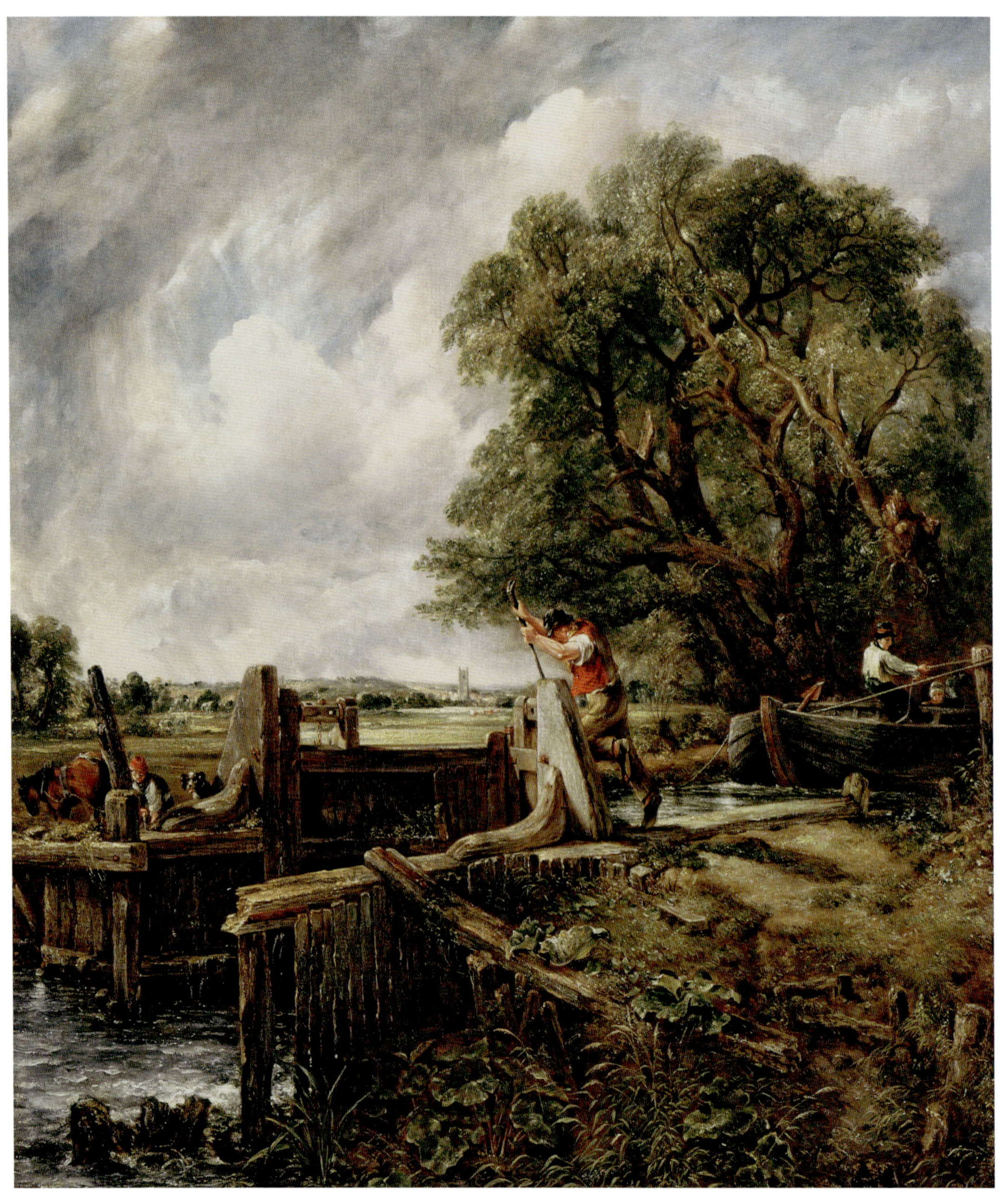

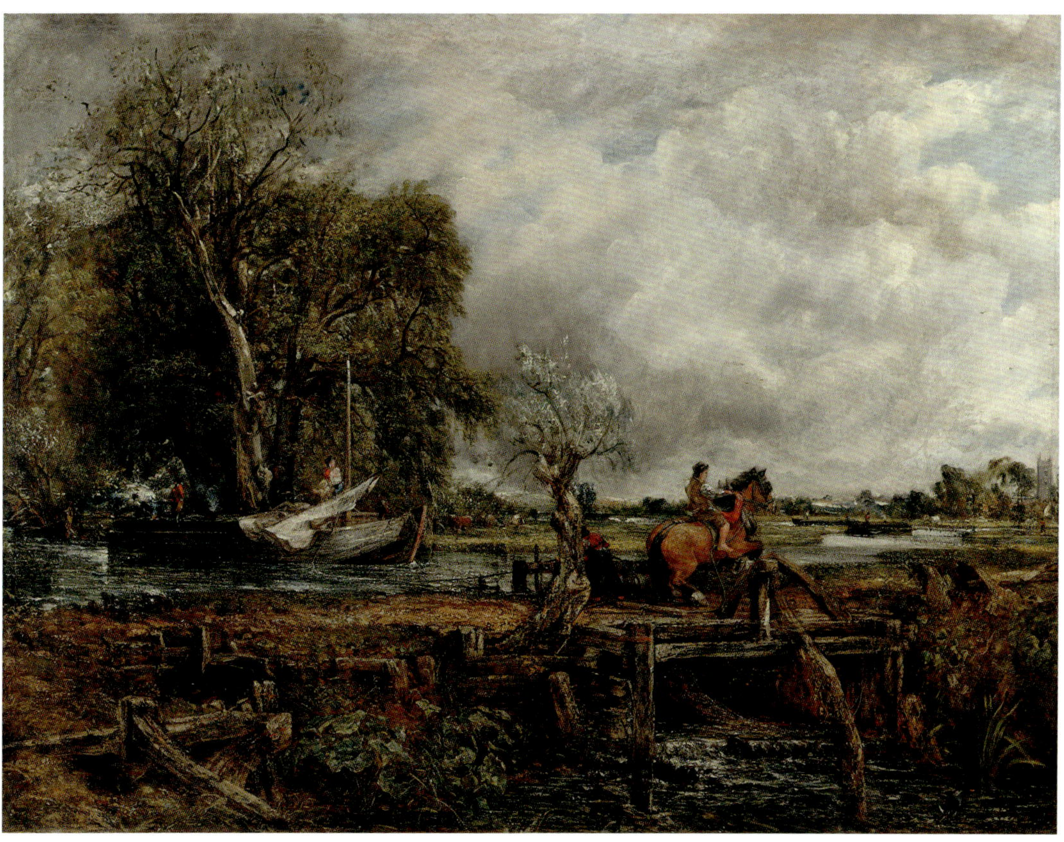

intended for submission to exhibitions) increasingly taking on the sketchy qualities of the preparatory works.

The White Horse was a definitive achievement and a turning point in Constable's career. It also represents a belated attempt by a middle-aged painter to establish his reputation and achieve financial security. It is now seen as the first of the celebrated series, but it is not clear that Constable initially planned to repeat the experiment. Following the success of *The White Horse* and *Stratford Mill*, in the autumn of 1820 Constable planned to present at the next Royal Academy exhibition a monumental painting of the celebration of the opening of Waterloo Bridge in London, which he had sketched in 1817. Unusually for him, the subject was urban, topical, and politically charged. But Constable struggled to complete the work and, following the advice of his friend and fellow artist Joseph Farington, returned instead to making and exhibiting the Stour paintings at the Royal Academy and establishing his reputation.[21]

Fig. 10
John Constable
The Lock, exh. 1824
Oil on canvas
56 × 47½ in. (142.2 × 120.7 cm)
Private collection

Fig. 11
John Constable
The Leaping Horse, exh. 1825
Oil on canvas
55⅞ × 73¾ in. (142 × 187.3 cm)
Royal Academy, London;
Given by Mrs. Dawkins 1889
(03/1391)

Waterloo Bridge haunted Constable's studio over the next decade.[22] He finally exhibited the definitive version of it in 1832 (fig. 12), causing a famous incident with Turner. During the "Varnishing Day" held just before the opening of the Academy exhibition and in response to passages of brilliant red in *Waterloo Bridge*, Turner added to his own submission, *Helvoetsluys* (fig. 13), a shocking and composition-resolving red buoy.[23]

In 1821, Constable presented *The Hay Wain* (see fig. 7)—his third scene of "timeless" everyday life on the Stour—which would become his most famous work. He created River Stour six-footers every year from 1819 to 1825, missing only 1823, when he was consumed with other commissions; then he stopped, turning to other subjects such as the beach at Brighton, where he stayed regularly from 1824 with his wife Maria, in an attempt to restore her failing health. The series had become a critical success, and all but one of the six paintings sold during his lifetime; nevertheless, it did not resolve his financial difficulties.[24] Indeed, as is so often the case, Constable's art acquired greater acclaim and became much more desirable to collectors after his death, at first in England and later in the United States.

Fig. 12
John Constable
The Opening of Waterloo Bridge ("Whitehall Stairs, June 18th, 1817"), exh. 1832
Oil on canvas
51⅛ × 85⅞ in. (130.8 × 218 cm)
Tate Britain, London; Purchased with assistance from the National Heritage Memorial Fund, the Clore Foundation, the Art Fund, the Friends of the Tate Gallery and others 1987 (T04904)

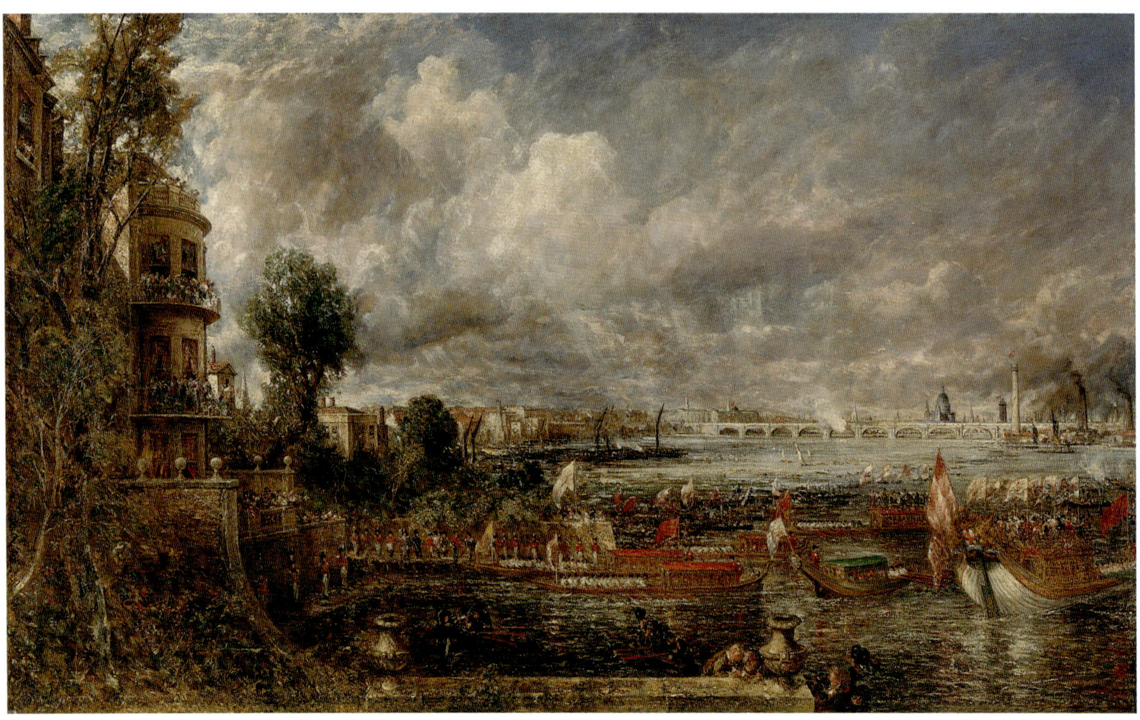

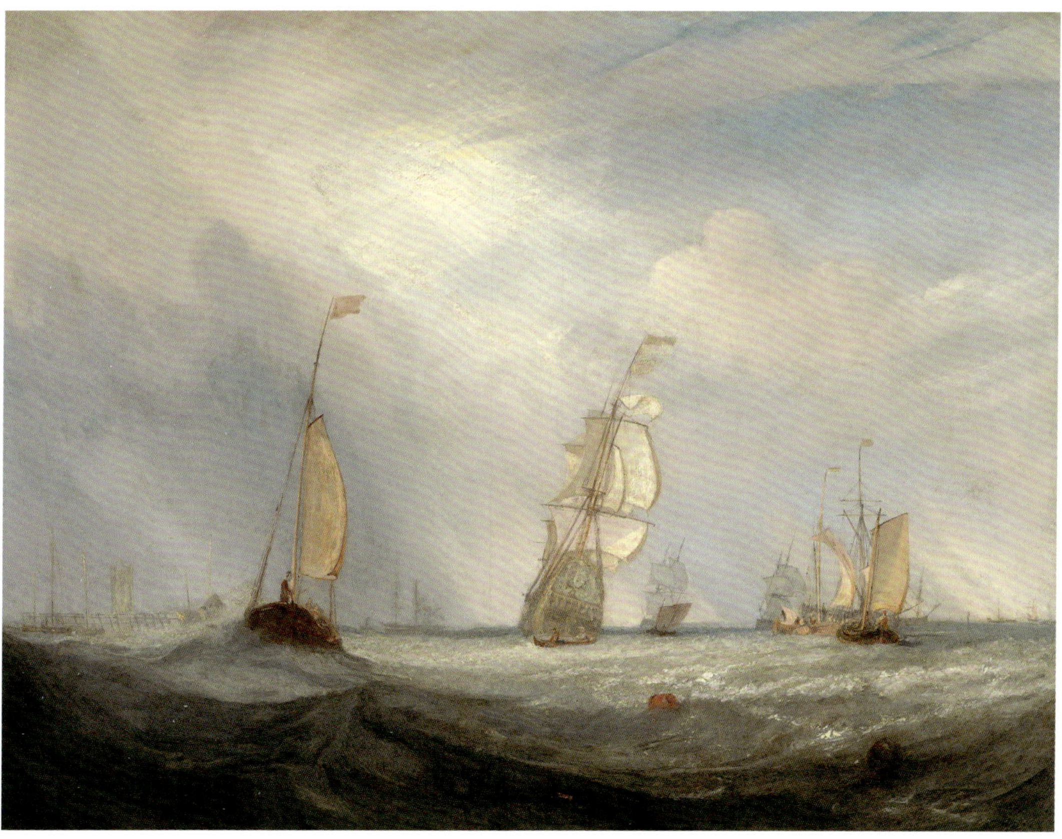

Fig. 13
J. M. W. Turner
Helvoetsluys—the City of Utrecht, 64, Going to Sea, exh. 1832
Oil on canvas
36 × 48 in. (91.4 × 122 cm)
Tokyo Fuji Art Museum

* * *

John Constable's career was one of struggle. His letters are rich with examples of his obstinacy and insecurity, his sometimes exasperating behavior. His father, Golding Constable (1739–1816), was a well-to-do merchant who fully or partially owned a number of mills in and around East Bergholt (fig. 17) and a transport business that operated vessels over navigable waterways to deliver produce to London.[25] The River Stour paintings commemorate these places and industries. As a young man aspiring to be a painter, John fought against the expectation that he would take over his father's businesses, a role filled eventually by his younger brother, Abram.[26] In 1799, John was able to move to London to enroll in art classes at the Royal Academy. His upper-middle-class status was helpful in securing access, but, in his correspondence through the 1810s and 1820s, he repeatedly refers to his need for money and his

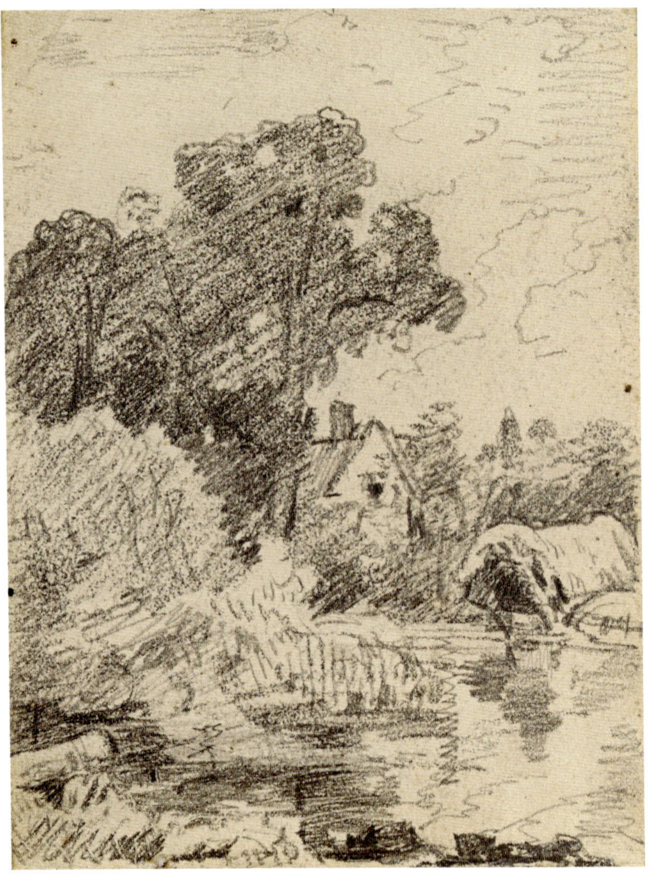

struggle for academic acceptance. By the time he was finally elected an associate member, in 1819, he was forty-three years old. It would be another decade before he attained full membership, and he did so by a margin of a single vote. To put Constable's career into perspective, Turner, who was just one year older, had been elected associate member and full member at ages twenty-four and twenty-six, respectively, and enjoyed early celebrity and wide commercial success. Turner had been a full member of the Royal Academy for seventeen years by the time Constable was elected as an associate.

Already during Constable's lifetime, the area in Suffolk depicted so often in his art was known as "Constable Country."[27] He painted on site in Suffolk for much of his early career and seems to have recorded these places with precision.[28] Like any artist, he also fictionalized elements of the landscape to suit his artistic needs.[29] The evolution of the white, red-roofed structure at the center of *The White Horse*, for example, illustrates how he modified a familiar landmark in Flatford. Known as Willy Lott's Cottage after the farmer (1761–1849) who inherited its tenancy in 1802 and then, in 1825, purchased it and the surrounding buildings, the cottage appears in a number of Constable's works, and in his correspondence he refers several times to painting it.[30] *The White Horse* approaches the cottage from the opposite side of the view that *The Hay Wain* eventually made iconic, and at a considerable distance. From what was probably the earliest drawing for the composition, made on site in a sketchbook in 1814 (fig. 14), to the exhibition painting now at the Frick (fig. 15), the structure of the cottage and its relationship to the surrounding trees changed. In the Frick painting, the cottage is seen through a more expansive clearing of trees and bears a stepped

Fig. 14
John Constable
Sketch of Willy Lott's Cottage, 1814
Pencil on paper
4¼ × 3⅛ in. (10.8 × 7.9 cm)
Victoria and Albert Museum, London; Given by Isabel Constable, daughter of the artist (1259-1888)

Fig. 15
John Constable
The White Horse, exh. 1819 (detail)

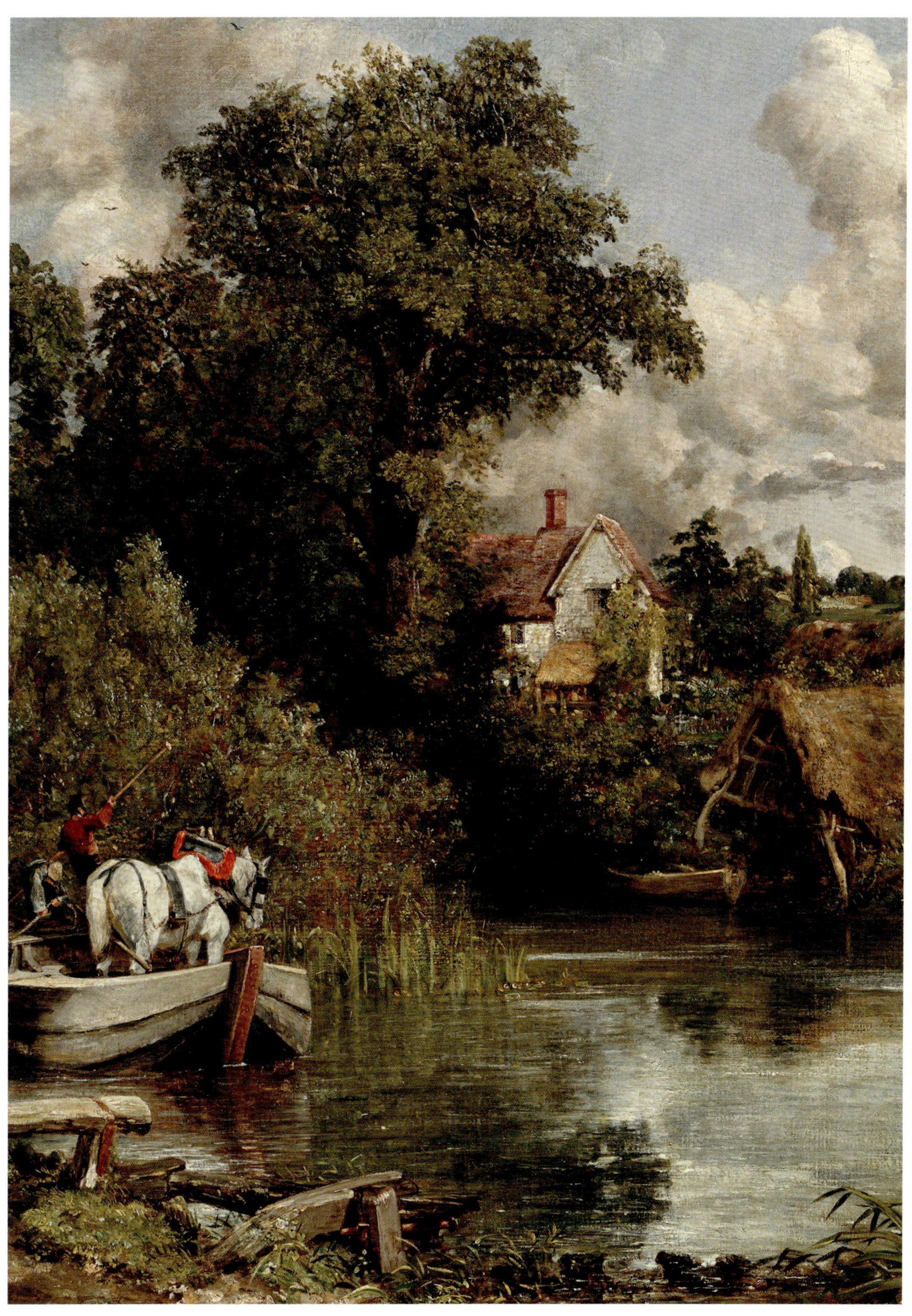

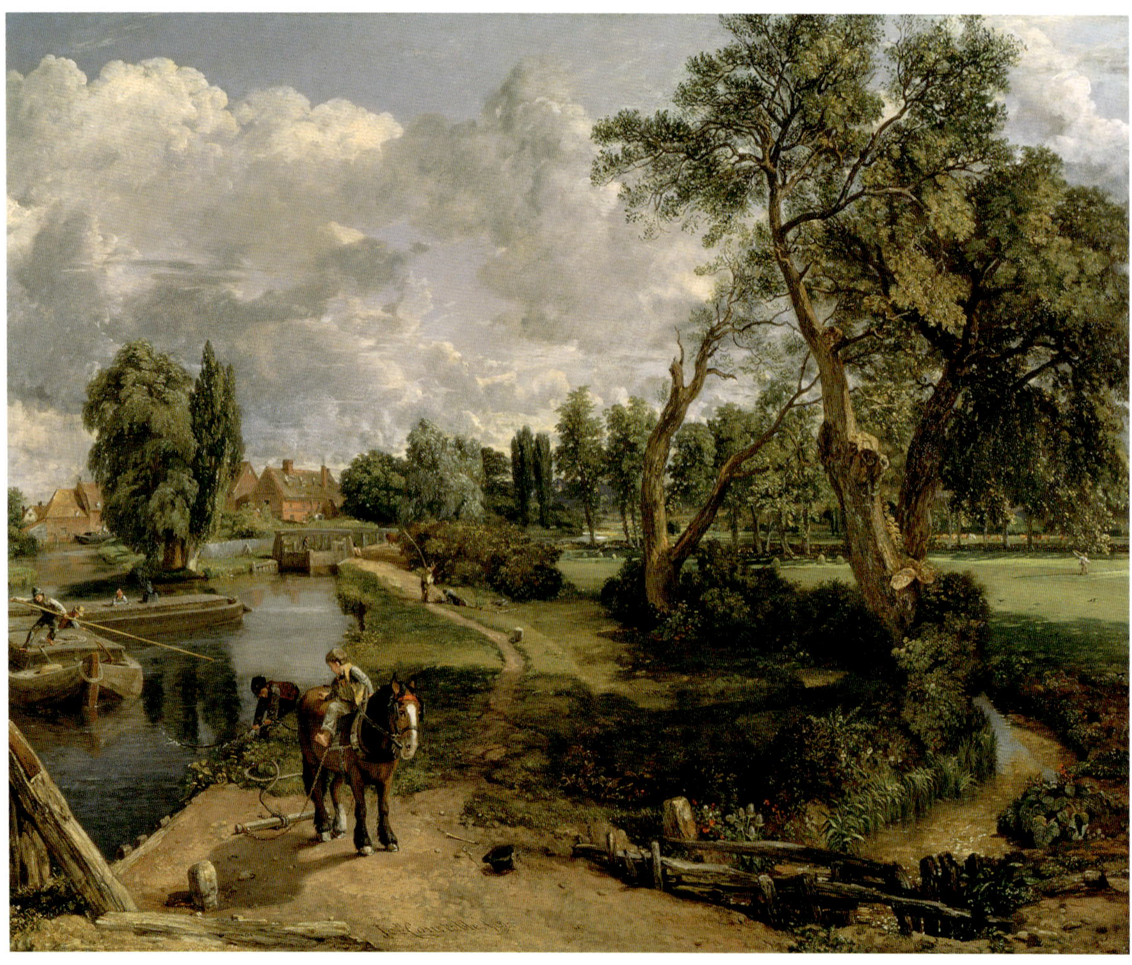

Fig. 16
John Constable
Flatford Mill ("Scene on a Navigable River"), exh. 1817
Oil on canvas
40 × 50 in. (101.6 × 127 cm)
Tate Britain, London; Bequeathed by Miss Isabel Constable as the gift of Maria Louisa, Isabel and Lionel Bicknell Constable 1888 (N01273)

roofline that does not correspond to Constable's other depictions of it or to the structure (since 1995 a Grade 1—"buildings of exceptional interest"—National Trust property) as it stands today. In the painting, the farmhouse to the right, partially obscured by trees, was known as Gibbonsgate Farm. At left, the barge passes a slender, leafy island called The Spong.

Constable showcases in his paintings his familiarity with horse-towed barge transport, one of his father's industries, which would eventually be made obsolete by steamboats, rail, and roads. In *Flatford Mill* (fig. 16), he shows a horse pulling a barge, or lighter, along the river, traveling on a towpath at the river's edge. *View on the Stour near Dedham* (see fig. 9) depicts traffic: two lighters pass a moored one oriented toward the opposite direction, while a horse waits on the far bank; bargemen and their families could live in house lighters (depicted with the small smoking chimneys in *View on the Stour near Dedham* and *Flatford Mill*), which contained cabins and trailed the cargo lighter.[31] *The Leaping Horse* (see fig. 11) depicts the sometimes dangerous moment when a barge horse had to jump over one of the gates or fences that periodically interrupted the towpath. In *The White Horse*, the horse is being transported across the water in the barge, as happened when the towpath switched to the other side at certain points along the waterways. The bargemen then had to push and steer the vessel, loaded with the horse and cargo, and Constable represents their exertion. The method required that the horses be trained to jump into and out of the barge, and, by the beginning of the twentieth century, the River Stour was the only waterway in England on which this method remained in use.[32]

* * *

Constable's full-size sketches for his monumental landscapes have captivated and mystified scholars, who have debated their precise roles and functions. How he came to produce his first full-size sketch is unknown (see fig. 4).[33] The six he did for the River Stour series vary—some are looser than others—and relate to their corresponding exhibition pictures in different ways. Their roles and functions in each case probably also varied. It is clear that they did not serve to establish final compositions—from which exhibition paintings derived with little change—as many details differ between sketches and paintings, and he made significant changes on the exhibition canvases. They seem instead to have developed in dialogue with the exhibition paintings, the two operating, to some extent, as alternate versions of a single composition.[34] When he worked with David Lucas to produce prints of his landscapes in the early 1830s, not having

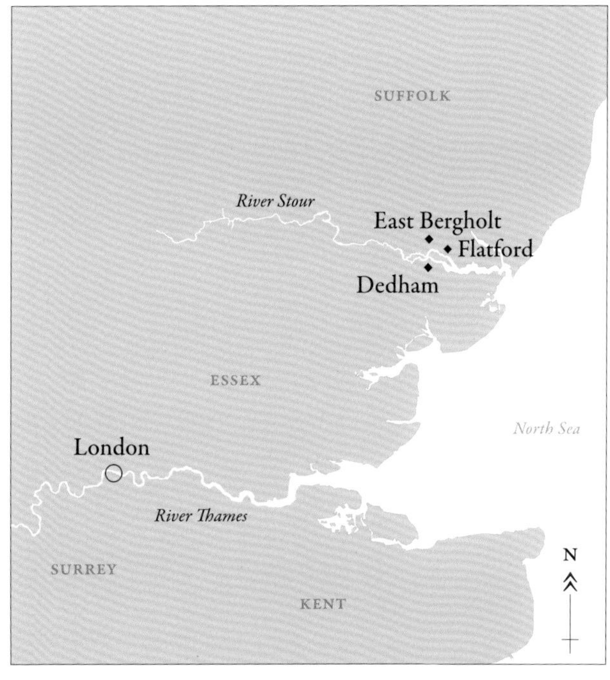

Fig. 17
Map showing London and the Suffolk towns in which Constable was active

the exhibition painting of *View on the Stour near Dedham* at hand (see fig. 9), he had Lucas engrave the full-size sketch instead (see fig. 8), even though the compositions are distinguished by the addition, in the exhibition painting, of a third lighter and other details.

Constable's friend and biographer C. R. Leslie reported that the artist made "sketches of the full size" for all of his large landscape paintings, but examples do not survive for all the known large-format landscapes.[35] Constable does not refer explicitly to the sketches, nor do any of his associates. The effect of seeing a full-size sketch side-by-side with the exhibition painting in Constable's studio—if this is indeed how he worked—must have been remarkable. The absence of any mention of them in Constable's copious correspondence raises questions about whether he deliberately kept them from view—and if so, how—and who during his lifetime saw them.

For the Stour series, the full-size sketch and corresponding exhibition painting of each pair are so close in scale and overall composition that Constable must have used a transfer method to establish the compositions on one canvas or the other (or both). No evidence suggests he used cartoons (full-size drawings on paper, sometimes with color, made to transfer a design to another support), which, widely used since the fifteenth century, offer one precedent for full-size preparatory works in European art. He appears to have used a grid to transfer his designs, tacking threads at evenly spaced intervals along the edges of his canvases.[36] The tacking edges of *The White Horse* have been trimmed, so it is not possible to determine if he used this method to transfer the composition to the canvas.[37]

Forgeries of Constable's oil sketches, some recognized as early as the decade after the artist's death, together with Constable's own copies and multiple versions of compositions, complicate the identification of autograph works.[38] Two smaller versions of *The White Horse* once thought to be preparatory works by Constable are now accepted as copies by unknown artists; formerly in notable collections, both are now untraceable.[39] Meanwhile, his full-size sketch now in the National Gallery of Art in Washington, D.C.—once considered a variant of the Frick painting—was dismissed by some as a copy until the late 1980s, when it was established that an unknown artist had overpainted an autograph work. When the Yale Center for British Art acquired the sketch for *Stratford Mill* in 1983, it had also been dismissed by some as a copy; revarnishing alleviated the doubts.[40]

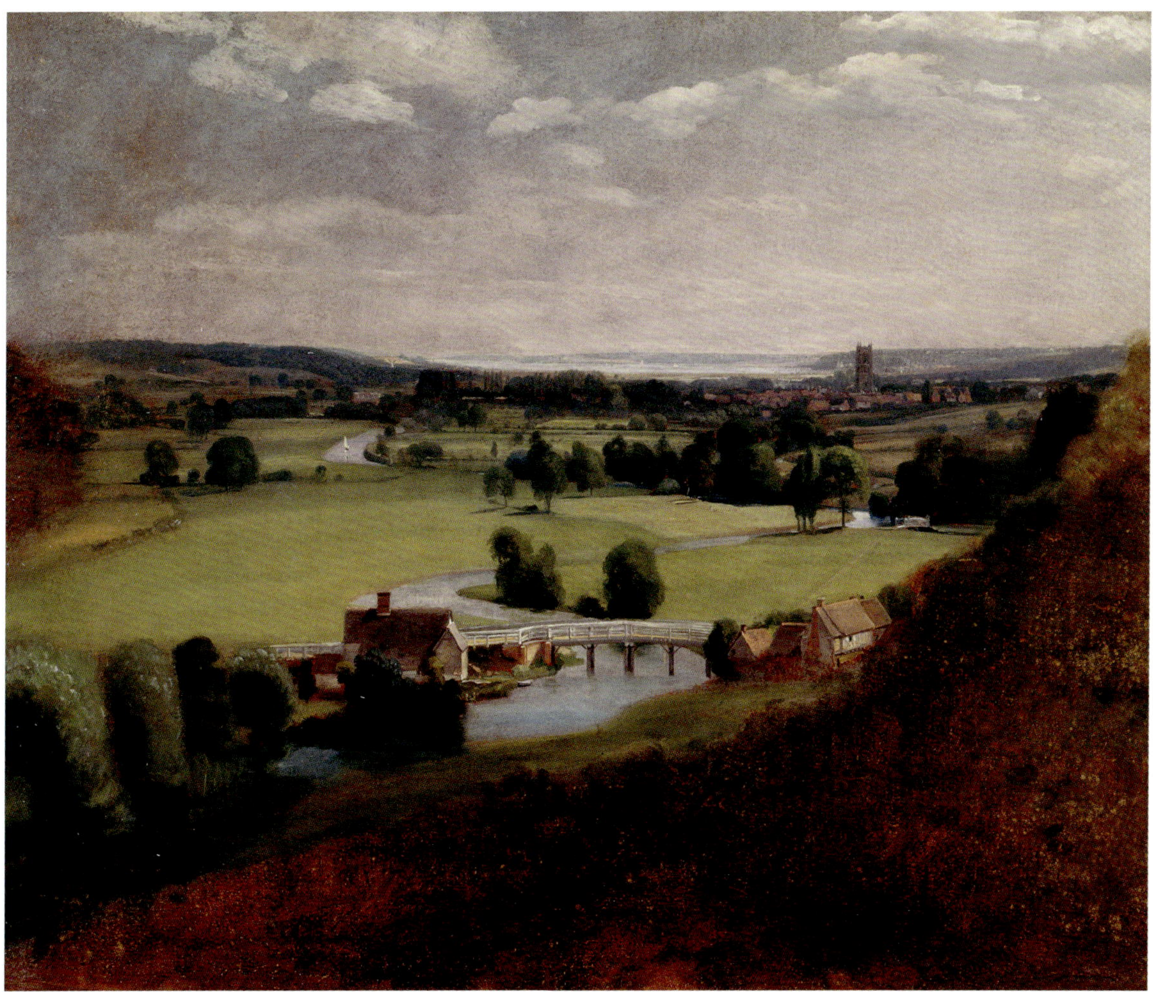

Fig. 18
John Constable
The Valley of the Stour with Dedham in the Distance ("View of Dedham Vale from the Coombs"), ca. 1800
Oil on paper laid on canvas
19⅝ x 23⅝ in. (49.8 × 60 cm)
Victoria and Albert Museum, London; Given by Isabel Constable (321-1888)

The full-size sketch for *The White Horse* cannot be identified with certainty among the lots in the 1838 sale of Constable's studio, but it was presumably among the artist's possessions when he died. As recorded in a print by Octave Jahyer dated 1883, at some point before this date an unknown artist heavily overpainted it in ways that made it appear more finished and closer in compositional details to the Frick picture (see fig. 5).[41] The earliest known reference to it was in 1872 (then in the collection of John Pender), when it was shown at the Royal Academy winter exhibition.[42] Whether or not it was already overpainted by this date is unknown. The accompanying catalogue gives no indication that it was not the canvas exhibited in 1819; evidently,

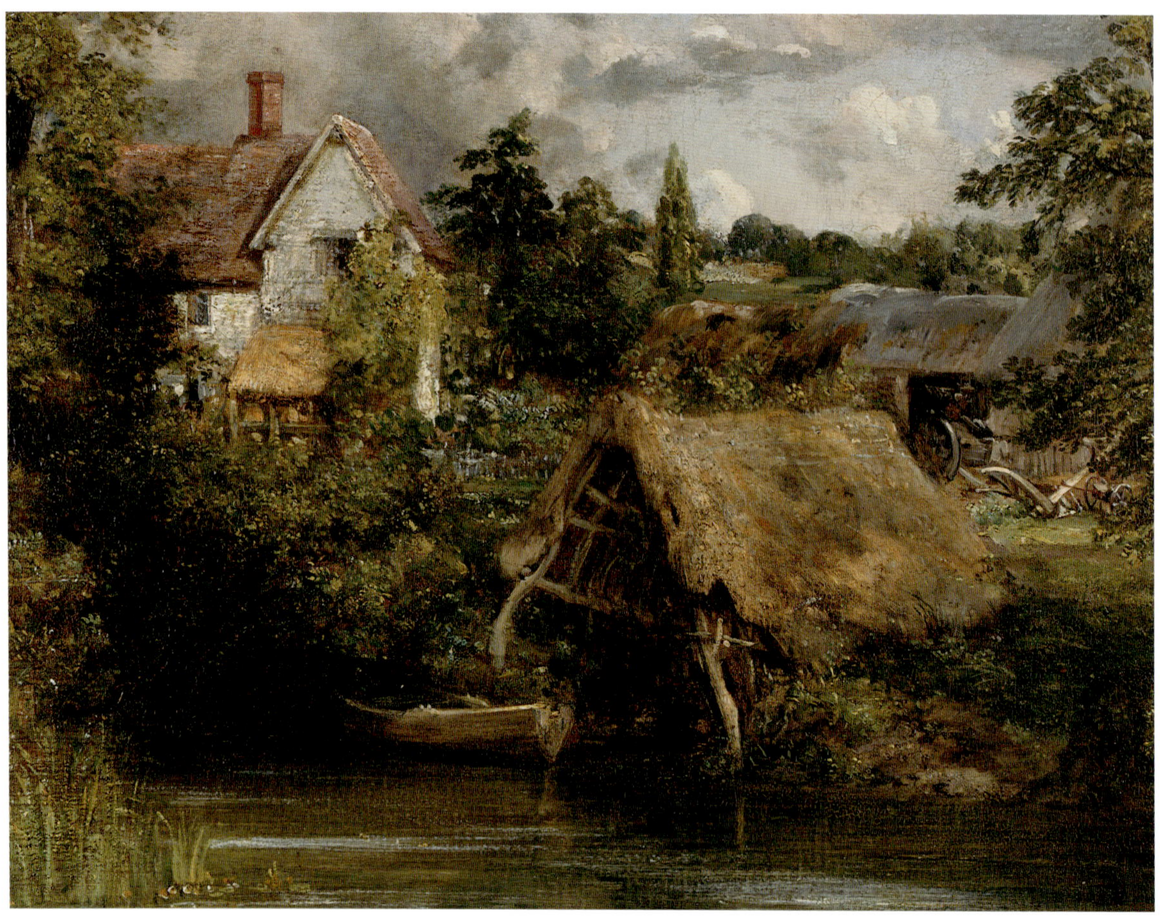

Fig. 19
John Constable
The White Horse, exh. 1819
(detail)

visitors were unaware that it was a different painting.[43] The American collector P. A. B. Widener acquired it in 1893. By the time it was given to the National Gallery of Art in the Widener bequest in 1942, there had been some suggestion that it might be a sketch for the Frick painting, but Robert Hoozee did not include it in his catalogue raisonné in 1979 ("very probably an imitation"), and the attribution remained a matter of debate.[44]

Its remarkable rediscovery in the late 1980s has been well published.[45] It was languishing in the conservation studio of the National Gallery of Art in 1984, when an X-radiography examination requested by Constable scholar Charles Rhyne revealed that it was painted on top of an entirely different composition. Rhyne identified the underlying composition as Constable's *Dedham Vale from the Coombs*, known in several versions (fig. 18).

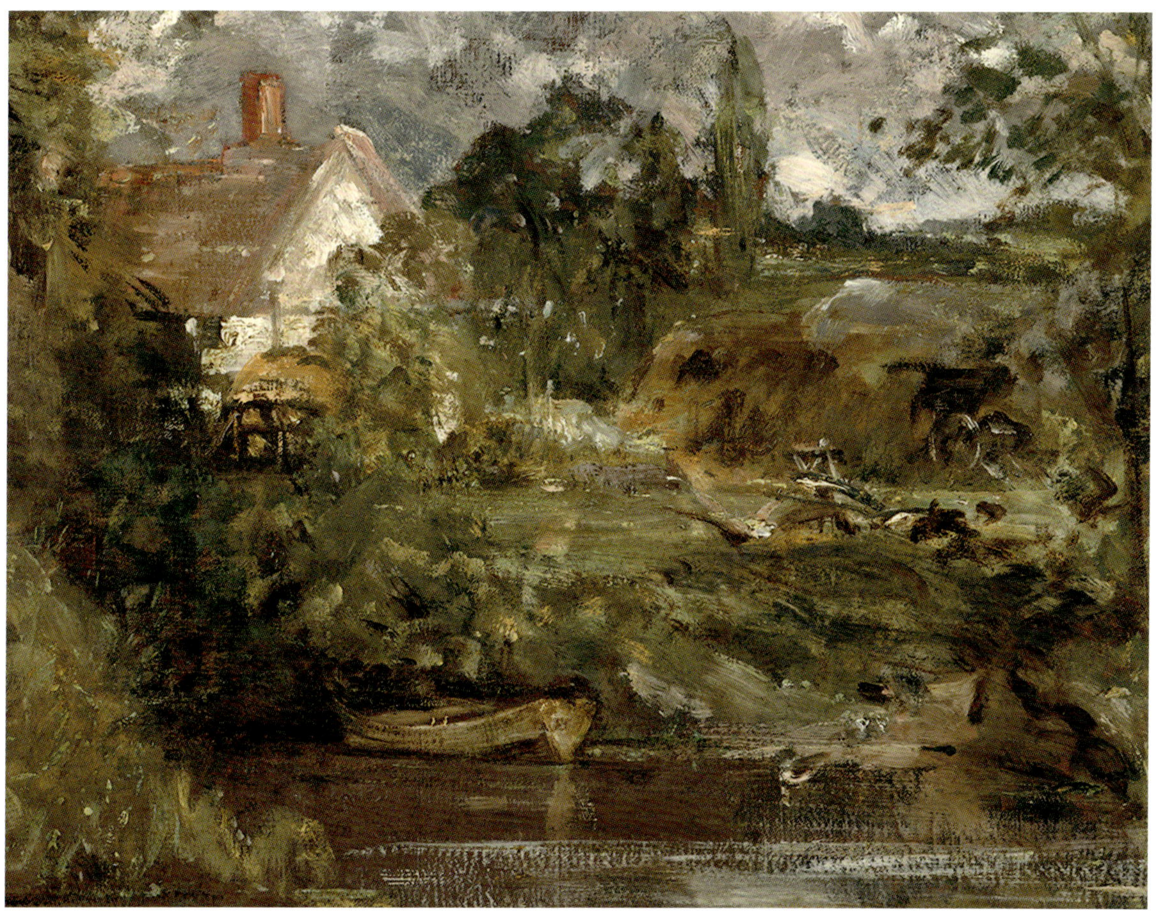

Fig. 20
John Constable
The White Horse (full-size sketch), 1818–19 (detail)

Interpretation of X-radiographs is especially challenging in cases like the Washington sketch in which one composition is painted over another; however, as it seemed highly unlikely that a copyist would paint a variant of *The White Horse* on top of another composition by Constable, its autograph status was confirmed. Constable may have even incorporated details from the abandoned *Dedham* composition into *The White Horse* sketch.[46]

Between 1992 and 1997, conservator Michael Swicklik identified and removed the extensive overpaint to reveal the sketch's loose, open brushwork and the surprising fact that Constable had not included the boathouse that features so prominently at the heart of the Frick painting (figs. 19, 20). Evidently, the Washington sketch offered a distinct compositional alternative. Swicklik's treatment brought to light the many differences between the

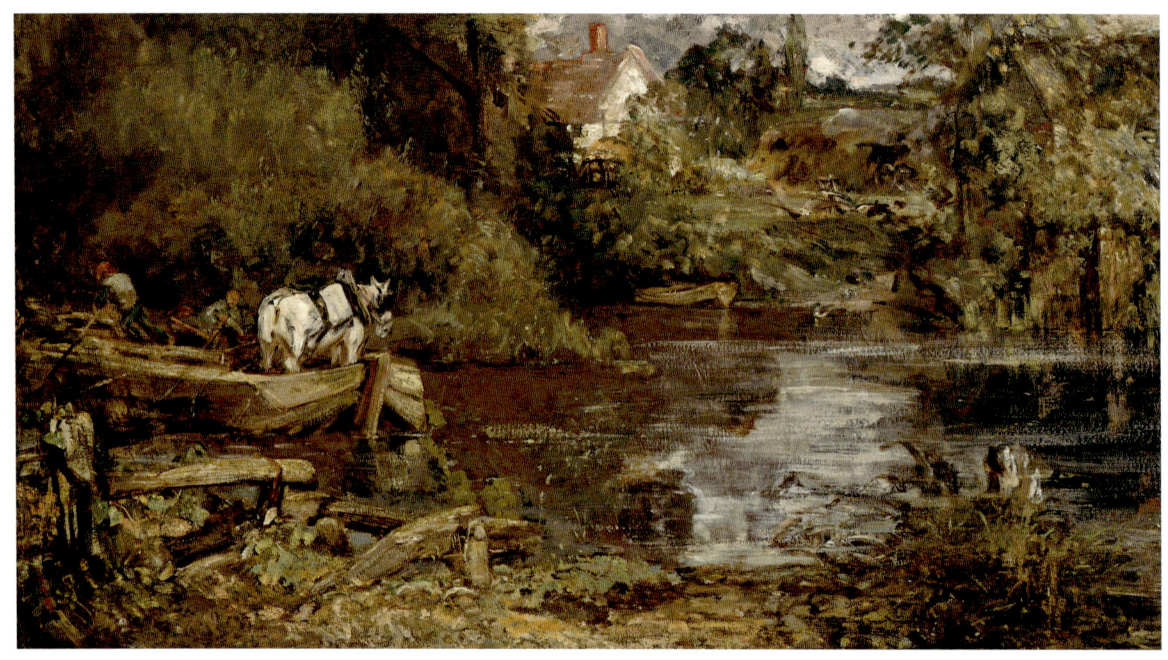

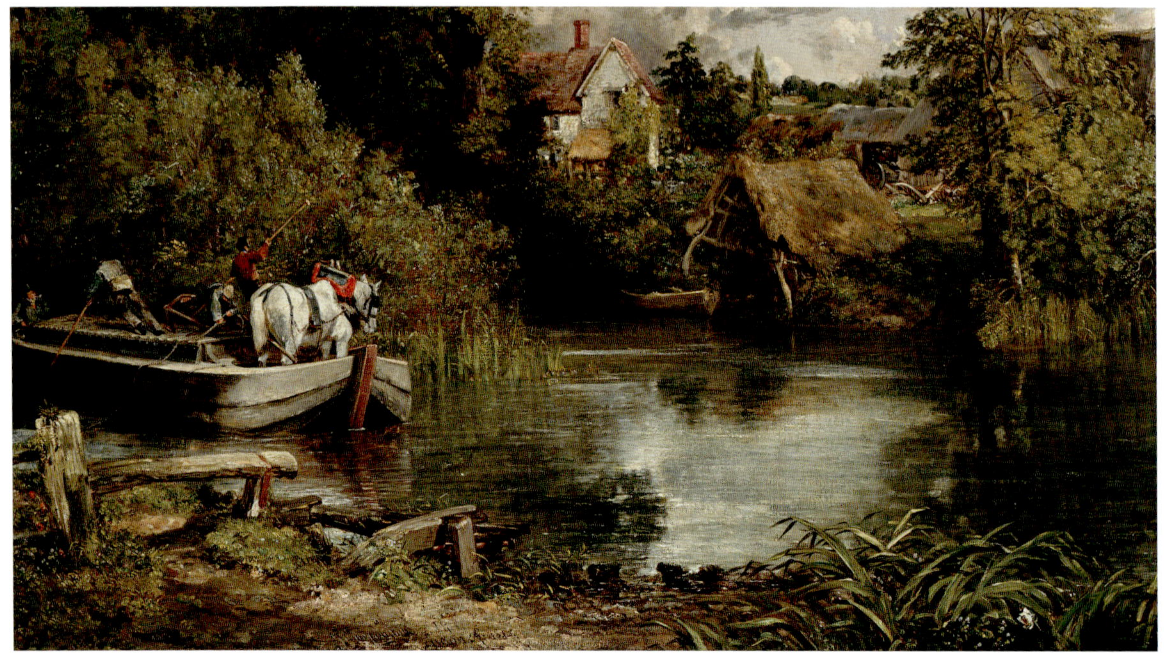

sketch and the exhibition painting. For example, in the sketch, in place of the boathouse a greater emphasis was given to the farmyard by the more central position of the plough, the prominence of the hay cart, and the "parading" of ducks or geese to the water's edge.[47] Four cows instead of three are in the water at right; a mooring in the foreground and a post in the middle ground to the left of the cows are absent in the Frick painting; and a different arrangement of the figures is on the barge. The group in the barge changed considerably in its details. Constable's solution in the Frick painting takes advantage of the contrast of red and white to draw attention to the group. It certainly compelled Fisher to take notice when he gave the painting its nickname. Regarding the abandoned *Dedham Vale from the Coombs* composition—which would have been Constable's largest exhibition painting before *The White Horse*—Swicklik's treatment revealed that it was more sketchy than finished; either it was a sketch or the artist did not get very far before abandoning it.[48]

In 2019, the first technical examination of the Frick painting was undertaken at the Metropolitan Museum of Art, making it possible to

Fig. 21
John Constable
The White Horse (full-size sketch), 1818–19 (detail)

Fig. 22
John Constable
The White Horse, exh. 1819 (detail)

Fig. 23
X-radiograph mosaic detail, presence of stretcher digitally reduced. The red arrow indicates the earlier position of the log of the gate, and the green arrows indicate the mooring and post, as seen in the full-size sketch, that were later painted out of the exhibition painting.

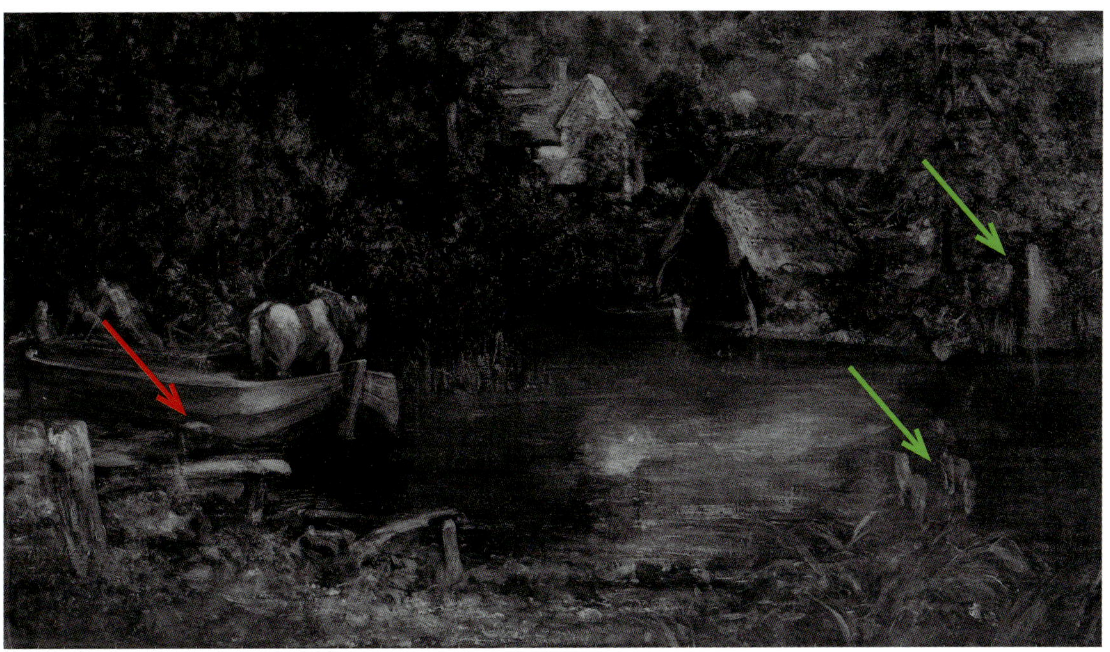

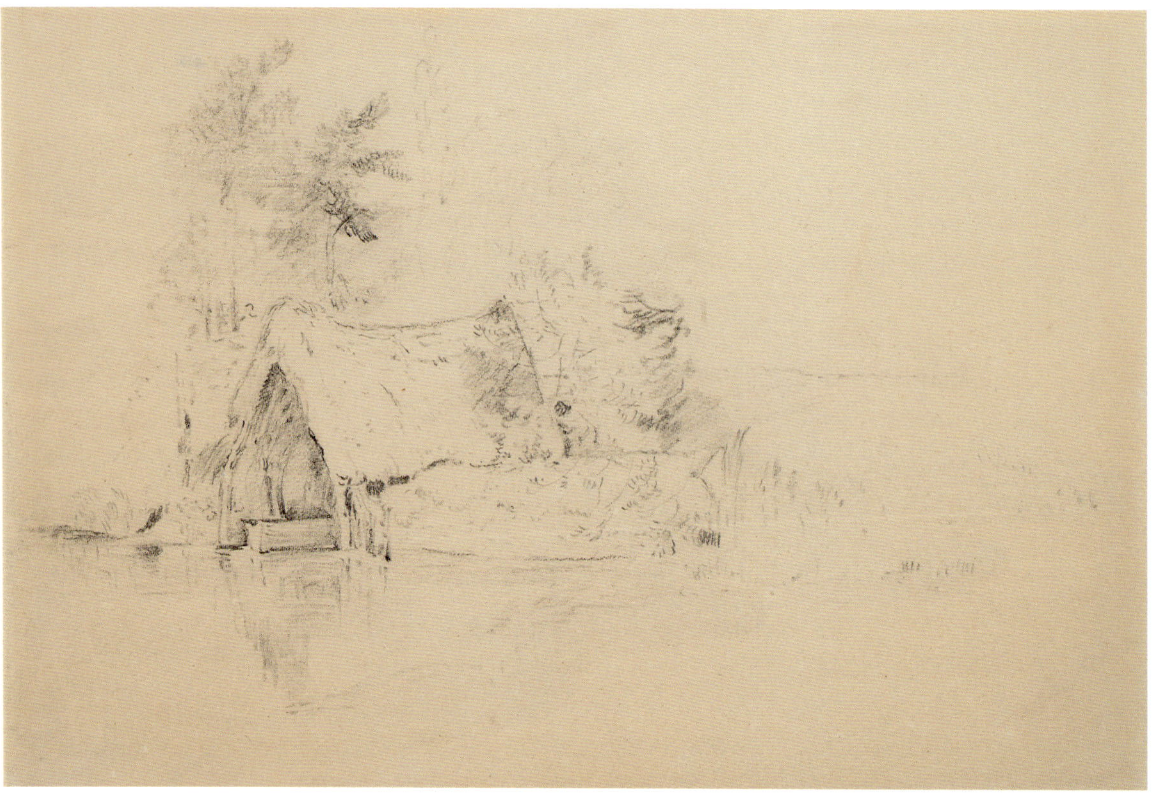

Fig. 24
John Constable
The Boat House at Flatford: A Study for "The White Horse,"
ca. 1817
Pencil on paper
7 3⁄16 × 10 7⁄8 in. (183 × 277 mm)
Private collection

understand more about its relationship to the Washington sketch.[49] They had previously shared more details. For instance, the mooring in the foreground and the post to the left of the cows present in the sketch were also once in the Frick painting (figs. 21–23). Constable created a more placid effect around the pond in the Frick picture by painting them out. The area around Willy Lott's Cottage has garnered particular scholarly interest because the dark form above it in the Frick painting has been interpreted by some (before technical examination) to be a pentimento.[50] A similar form appears above the cottage in the Washington sketch.[51] Examination through X-radiography and infrared reflectography did not provide enough information from which to draw definitive conclusions about the dark form—or about scraping marks apparent in the X-radiograph of the Frick painting on either side of the chimney which indicate that Constable made some kind of change.

Ongoing technical study is continuing to clarify the relationships among the Washington sketch, the Frick painting, and associated small-scale preparatory works.[52] These include the sketchbook drawing of 1814 (see fig. 14),[53] two drawings of the boathouse and a boat (figs. 24, 25),[54] and three oil sketches: a vertical sketch for the area around Willy Lott's Cottage, a horizontal sketch of a similar view datable to the summer of 1816, and one for the barge that came to light in the early twenty-first century (figs. 26–28).[55] Constable often drew from and combined a number of preparatory works for a single composition.[56]

Results of the recent examination underline the importance of the sketchbook drawing (see fig. 14) for the Frick painting, which derives in part—and possibly directly—from it. From the outset, the painting seems to have included the boathouse in its composition, for no articulated landscape (such as a clearing with ducks or geese, as seen in this area in the Washington sketch) is apparent beneath the boathouse in the X-ray. The long log at the lower left corner of the Frick painting was first painted at a more oblique angle, as in the sketchbook drawing (see figs. 14, 15); presumably, Constable adjusted its angle to avoid its overlapping the barge, and he also moved the post slightly to the right. The available evidence

Fig. 25
John Constable
Rowing Boat Moored beneath a Bank, ca. 1809–11
Black chalk on blue-gray paper
3½ × 5 in. (90 × 126 mm)
Courtauld Institute of Art Gallery, London; Sir Robert Clermont Witt bequest, 1952 (D.1952.RW.3943)

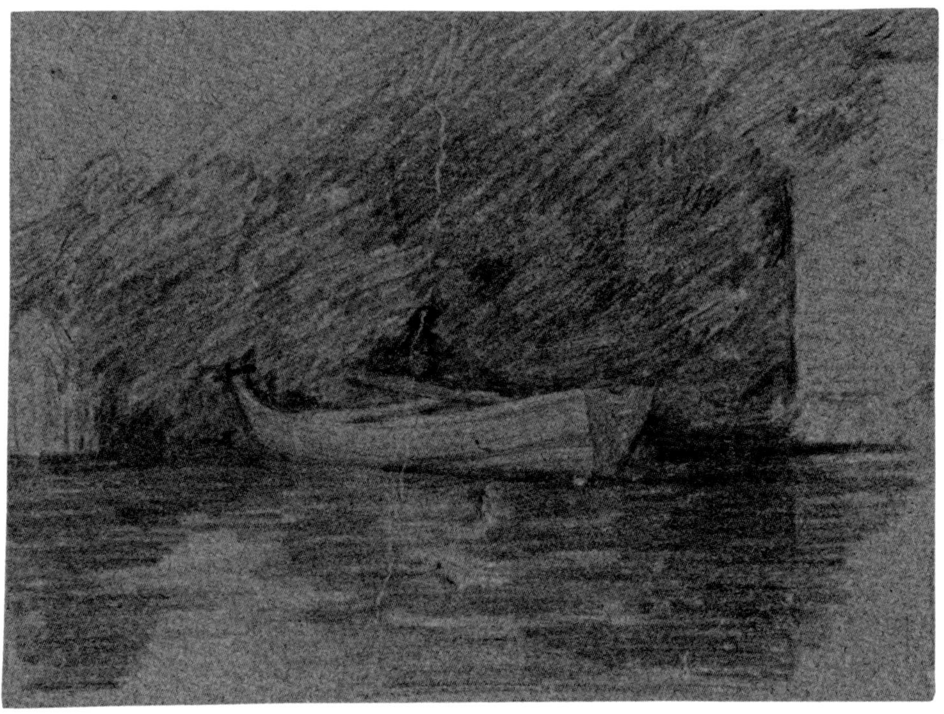

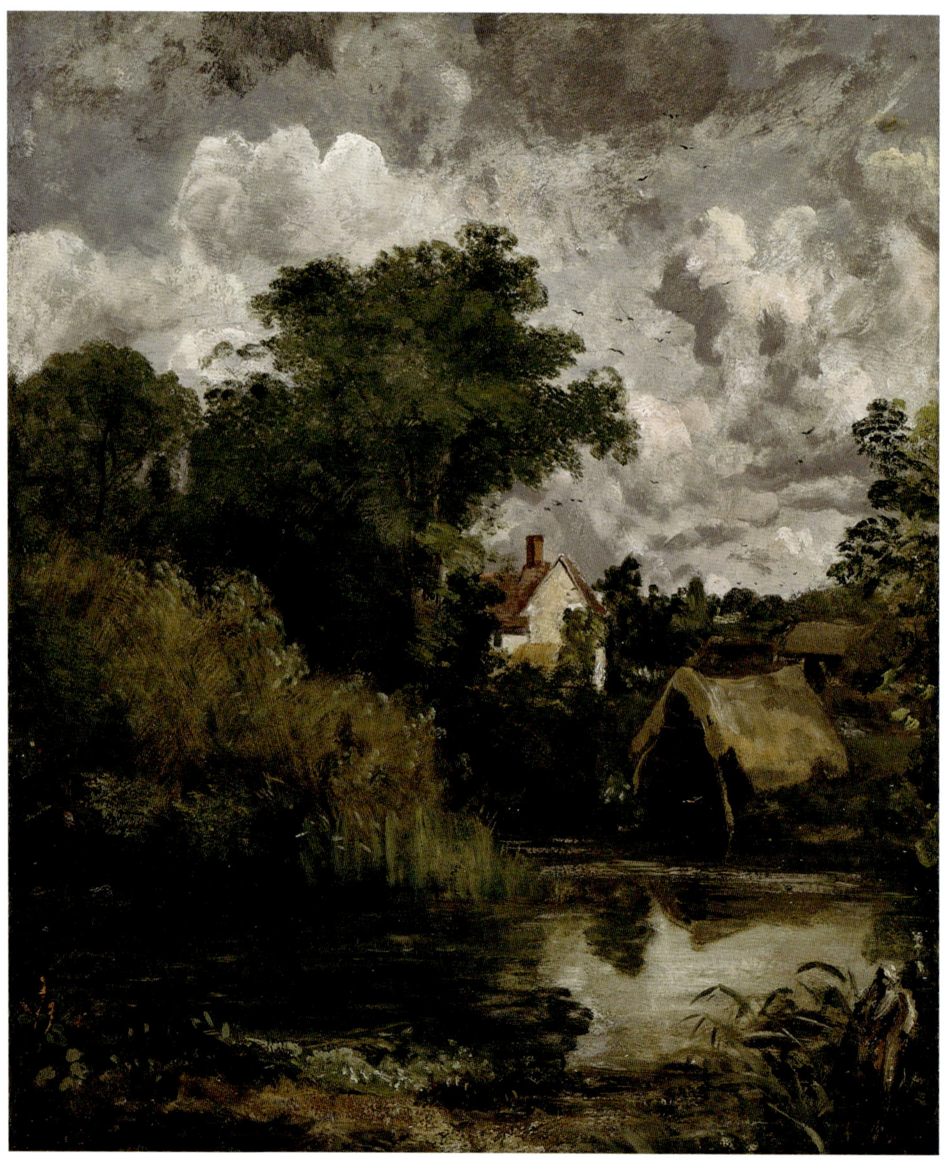

suggests that the Washington sketch always included the "corrected" angle of the fence. This may suggest that the full-size sketch was initiated *after* Constable had already started the Frick painting, contrary to the traditional sequence of making a sketch before the exhibition painting. Perhaps he picked up the abandoned exhibition canvas (with the *Dedham Vale* composition) to test out an alternate version of *The White Horse*, at the same scale, without the

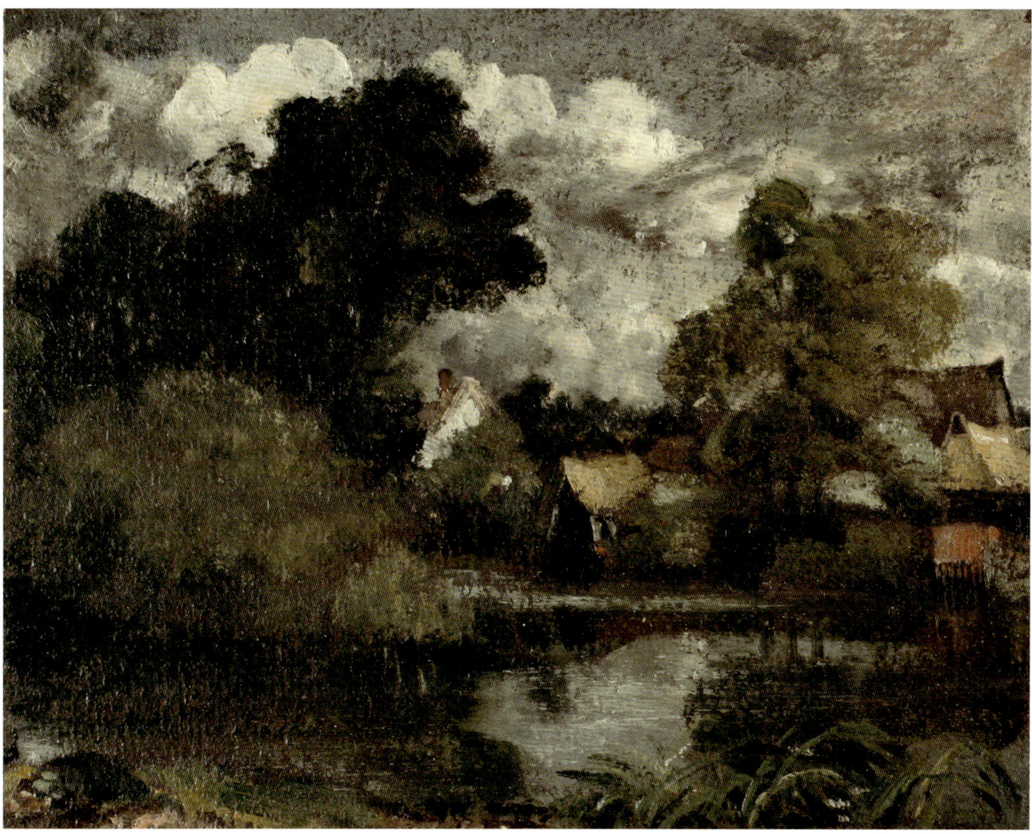

central boathouse. Clearly, he found a full-size sketch useful enough to repeat the process for the five subsequent Stour paintings, presumably initiating each sketch before, or perhaps at the same time as, the exhibition picture. One art historian questioned whether the full-size sketches were rejected solutions abandoned early, full-scale *modelli*, or alternate versions kept in progress with the others in which alternative possibilities could be tested.[57] The recent examination suggests that, at least for the first full-size sketch, the latter was most probably correct.

Sketching and painting *en plein air* was an important part of Constable's practice throughout his career, and a number of the preparatory works associated with *The White Horse* appear to have been made on site during one or more of his various sketching trips. His faith in direct observation of subjects led him to protest the formation of the National Gallery in London because he was concerned that young artists would go there to study paintings

Fig. 26
John Constable
Study for "The White Horse," 1817
Oil on canvas
24 × 19¾ in. (61 × 50 cm)
Private collection

Fig. 27
John Constable
Study for "The White Horse," 1816
Oil on canvas
9¼ × 11⅞ in. (23.5 × 30.2 cm)
Private collection

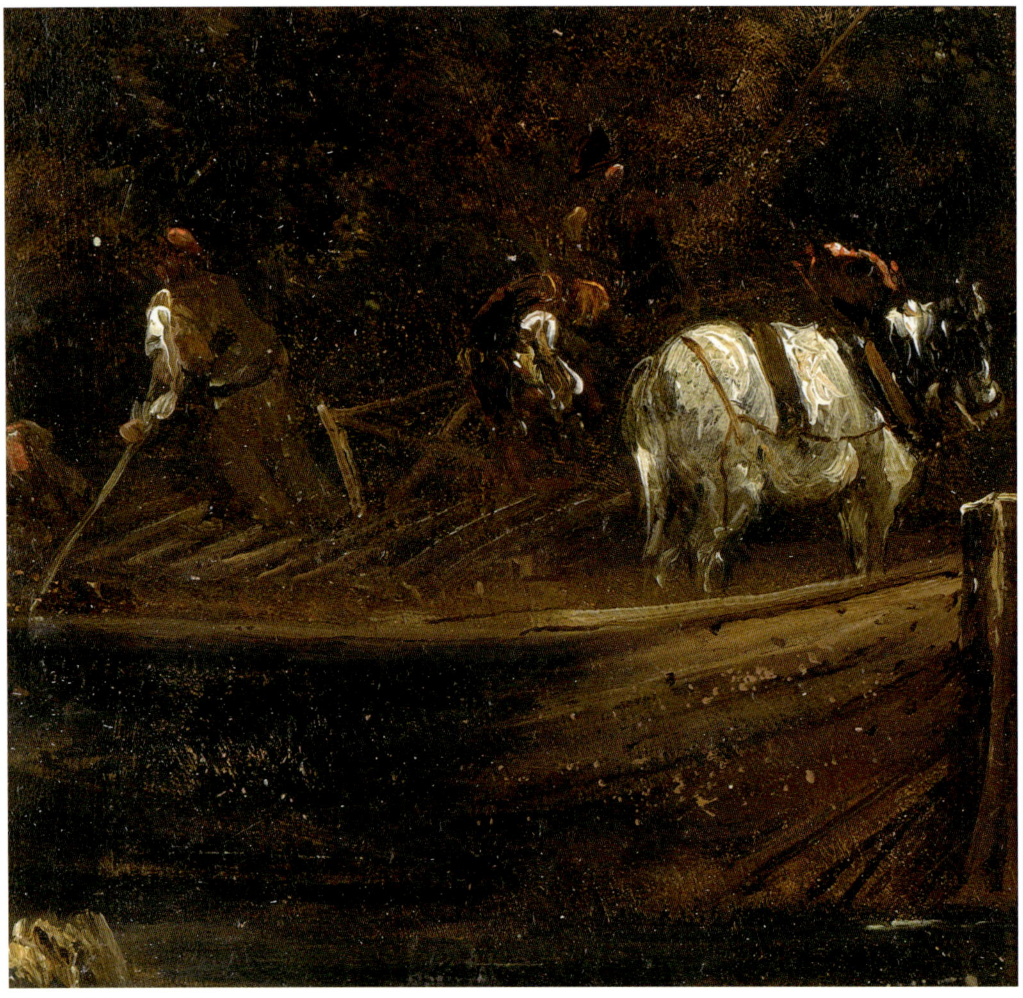

Fig. 28
John Constable
Study of Men and Tow-Horse on Barge, ca. 1818–19
Oil on millboard
5¼ × 5¾ in. (13.4 × 14.5 cm)
Private collection

and thereby abandon studying objects in nature with their own eyes.[58] Scholars have proposed that he painted *Flatford Mill* (see fig. 16), the largest painting he exhibited before *The White Horse*, in large part *en plein air*.[59] About thirty centimeters taller and sixty wider, *The White Horse* and the subsequent six-footers presumably would have been too large to execute outdoors without great difficulty. Painting *The White Horse* relied on the transport to his London studio of drawings and sketches made on site in Suffolk; like the barge in the painting, his sketchbooks, loose sheets, and portable oil sketches operated as vessels transporting elements of the Stour Valley to London.

* * *

A major challenge to understanding Constable's working process is that he continued to work on his paintings after they were exhibited and sometimes returned to them years later.[60] He also expressed a belief that his paintings continued to change even without his involvement, that natural processes had a role in developing his works even after they left his studio. He described the effects of air on his paints, saying that his landscapes would take on their ideal appearance after about one year.[61] In this way, the responsive physical properties of his paintings echoed the natural processes he sought to capture in them.

Before the opening of their exhibitions, the Royal Academy held "Varnishing Days" so that artists could make finishing touches to and varnish their submissions; like many others, Constable appears to have taken advantage of this system by submitting works that were not entirely finished. He seems to have struggled generally with completing his works; throughout his career, he made references to the challenge of finishing.[62] According to Fisher, some were also concerned that he had the capacity to "destroy" a completed painting if it returned to his easel. Fisher reported to Constable the concerns of Tinney, the owner of *Stratford Mill*—"he dreads you touching the picture."[63] These concerns might explain Tinney's resistance to allowing Constable to submit *Stratford Mill* for exhibitions abroad; he may have feared that Constable would also put it back on his easel.[64]

After the exhibition of *The White Horse* in 1819, Fisher encouraged Constable to continue working on the painting, suggesting that he knew a buyer who would be interested should the painting be improved; the buyer turned out to be Fisher himself.[65] Constable certainly modified it after the exhibition, but it is not known what his changes were. No contemporary text provides sufficient detail to determine its precise appearance at the 1819 exhibition. He later added or amended the inscription at the bottom of the painting—*John Constable ARA/ London f[ecit] 1819*—as the "ARA" (Associate Member of the Royal Academy) could only have been added after his election in November of that year.[66]

As if to highlight the notions of place, distance, and transport embedded in the painting, Constable included in this inscription the name of a place that is not depicted, apparently for the first time in his career. He inscribed numerous works with names of places, seemingly implying that the drawing or painting was made at that site.[67] In *The White Horse*, "London" acknowledged the place of production, while the original exhibition title (*Scene on the River Stour*) identified the represented site. Naming London as the place of production associated Constable with England's artistic center and drew attention to the achievement of having painted an image of convincing naturalism away from the site itself. At the same time, as has been suggested, signing the canvas from London intimated an element of retrospect.[68]

In another related drawing, in the Fitzwilliam Museum, Constable revisits *The White Horse* composition and encases it within a generalized frame design inscribed with dimensions—"four feet six inches" across and "three feet three inches" up the left edge—that are about two-thirds the size of the Frick painting (fig. 29). It seems to be a drawing for a framer, perhaps, as has been proposed, to frame a reduced copy of *The White Horse*; the copy formerly in the Museum of Fine Arts, Boston, has dimensions close to those inscribed on the drawing and has been suggested as a possible candidate painted perhaps by Constable's assistant, John Dunthorne.[69] The drawing may have been made to frame an entirely different composition, the image of *The White Horse* filled in by Constable as a fanciful memory of it.[70] An inscription on the verso of the drawing, also in the artist's hand, seems to refer to the dimensions for a case ("6.2 in / 4.8 case") that would suit the Frick painting, which traveled a fair amount during Constable's lifetime. The precise function—or functions—of the Fitzwilliam drawing remains a mystery.

Yet even in this small, seemingly utilitarian drawing—the interior composition having the appearance of a quickly executed *ricordo*—the artist takes the time to articulate in varied tones the difference between bulging trees and rolling clouds, to indicate reflections in the water and the vegetation at the water's edge (although no cows appear). The horse takes on a grander measure within the frame, its whiteness emphasized by reinforcing strokes of dark wash around it. It suggests that by this point Fisher had already nicknamed the painting, thereby inflating the significance of the animal within the scene.

In December of 1824, five years after exhibiting *The White Horse*, Constable wrote to Fisher requesting that he send him the painting without the frame so he could "do something to it, to nourish it."[71] One wonders if Fisher worried about the damage he might do. Upon its return from Lille in 1826, Constable's assistant, John Dunthorne, revarnished it, and Fisher found it "wonderfully improved."[72] He also mentions sending back to Constable an

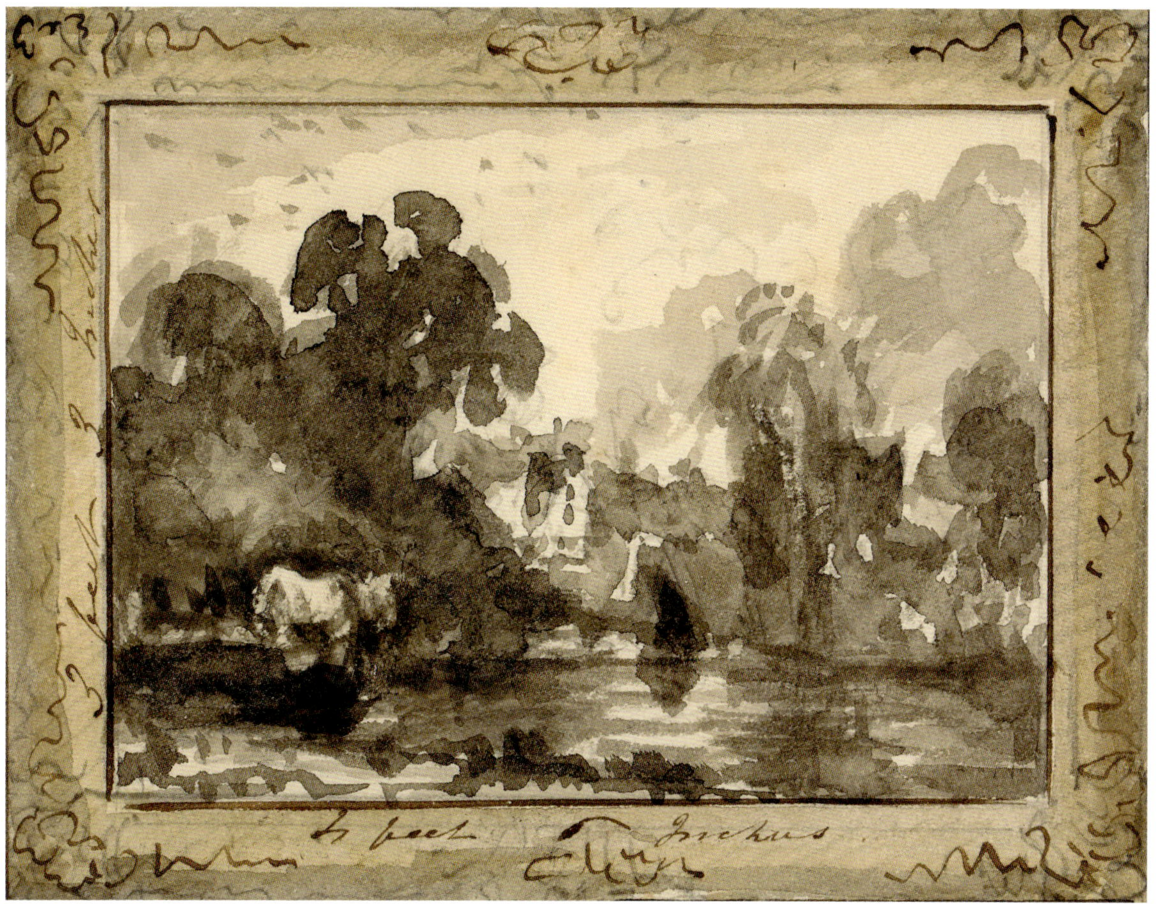

Fig. 29
John Constable
Sketch for the frame for "The White Horse," 1819
Graphite and ink on paper with gray wash
4 ¼ × 5 ⅝ in. (109 × 143 mm)
Fitzwilliam Museum, Cambridge (899.8)

"old frame."[73] Perhaps Constable ordered a new frame for the painting before sending it to France for exhibition. It is uncertain when, from whom, and how many frames he commissioned for the Frick painting and if the painting's current frame is the original one. Fisher's price of one hundred guineas for the painting did not include the frame.[74] In any case, the Fitzwilliam drawing seems to record Constable reimagining *The White Horse* composition, possibly from memory.

Elements of *The White Horse* have afterlives in subsequent River Stour paintings. The moored boat at center—probably also modeled after the detailed study now in the Courtauld (see fig. 25)—reappears nearly exactly at far right in *The Hay Wain* (see fig. 7). This offers some insight into Constable's working processes, in which sketches and drawings were retained for years to be incorporated into multiple compositions. In *View on the Stour near Dedham* (see fig. 9), exhibited in 1822, a white horse nearly identical to the one in the Frick painting appears behind the moored barge at left. Whether or not these self-referential elements were intended to be recognized by others is an open question. Both paintings were shown at the Paris Salon in 1824 and together won the artist a gold medal.[75]

Sometime around 1830, Constable engaged the mezzotint engraver David Lucas to reproduce some of his representative landscapes, including some oil sketches, in a series of publications called *English Landscape*, in which he also included remarks on his artistic practice and theories.[76] Lucas's task of translating Constable's paintings into monochromatic mezzotints was challenging, especially since color played a fundamental part in the naturalism of the landscapes. As Delacroix recounted, for example, Constable boasted that the superiority of his green lay in its being composed of a multitude of different greens.[77] However, mezzotint was an effective medium for conveying light and shadow—the "chiaroscuro" of nature—central to Constable's practice. The production of Lucas's printing plates may be considered a further step in the evolution of Constable's compositions, for he exercised control over them through "touched proofs," marking up multiple proofs prepared by Lucas sometimes to the point of radically altering the composition.[78] At times, Constable had Lucas work directly from the paintings he was translating into print, with Lucas often carrying them by hand as he walked the short distance between his studio and Constable's.[79] Lucas had *The White Horse* in his studio in 1831 and probably had initiated his print after it by August. Seven working proofs have been identified, the subtle differences among them seeming to indicate the minuteness of Constable's adjustments.[80] Around this time, Constable seems to have changed the way he thought about the painting, as he appears to give it an alternate title—*Farm Yard*—curiously effacing Fisher's emphasis on the horse and highlighting the function of the farmyard, as the full-scale sketch does.[81] Ultimately, Constable, notoriously demanding of Lucas, was dissatisfied with the print, and it was not published during his lifetime.[82]

Constable dissolved the partnership with Lucas in 1833, with the series incomplete and having made little profit; Constable called it a "total failure & loss."[83] In 1838, a year after Constable's death, Lucas worked with the publisher F. G. Moon to publish six plates, including *The White Horse* (fig. 30), though whether or not the prints were issued in 1838 or just lettered with that date is

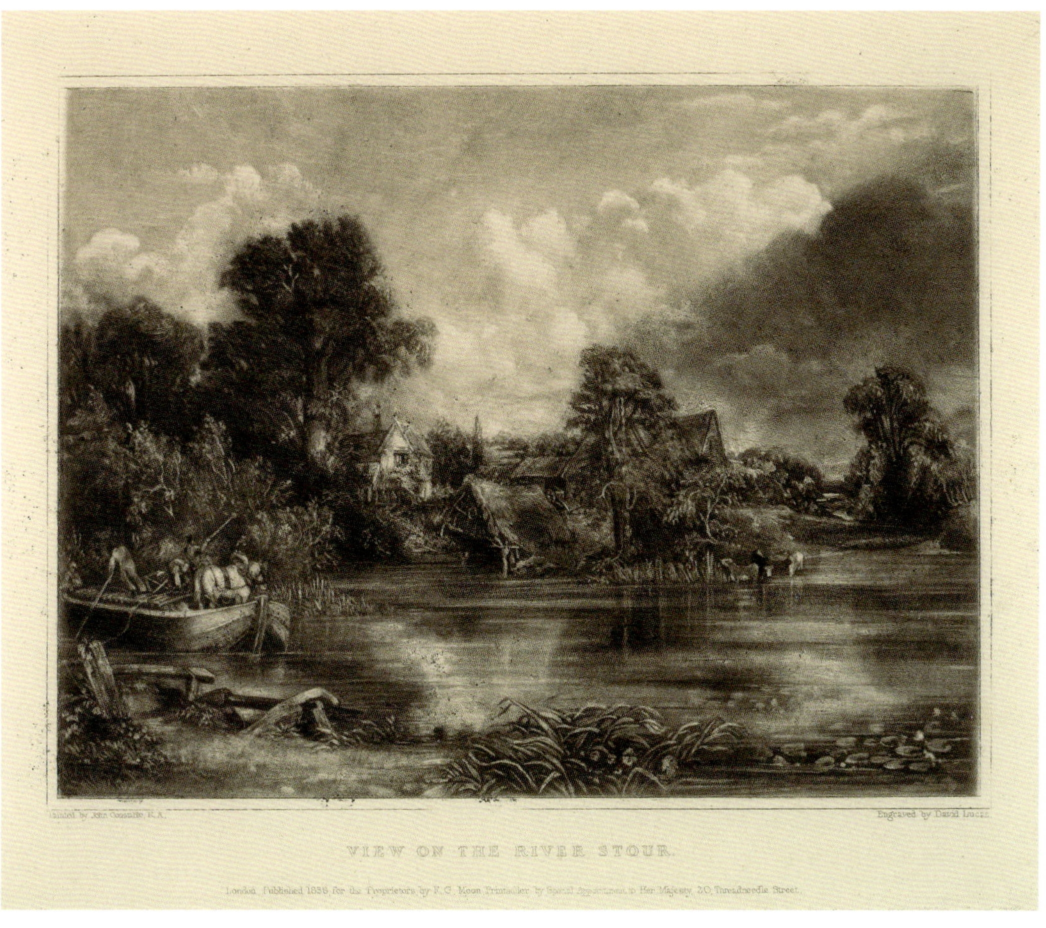

Fig. 30
David Lucas, after John Constable
View on the River Stour (The White Horse), dated 1838
Mezzotint
15½ × 13¾ in. (39.4 × 34.9 cm)
The Frick Collection, New York; Purchased by The Frick Collection, 1968 (1968.3.102)

uncertain.[84] On one proof of *The White Horse*, Leslie (who was supervising the project) inscribed, "This is the most famous of Constable's pictures & wants particular attention."[85] Like all Constable's endeavors in printmaking, the project drew scant attention and met with little commercial success.

* * *

During its return from Lille in the winter of 1826, *The White Horse* got held up in transit. As Constable wrote to Fisher on January 14, "Your paintings are in the river—where they must wait on board 'till the ice breaks."[86] It is unclear which other painting Constable refers to or if the reference to more than one picture was an error.[87] *The White Horse* arrived safely at Fisher's home

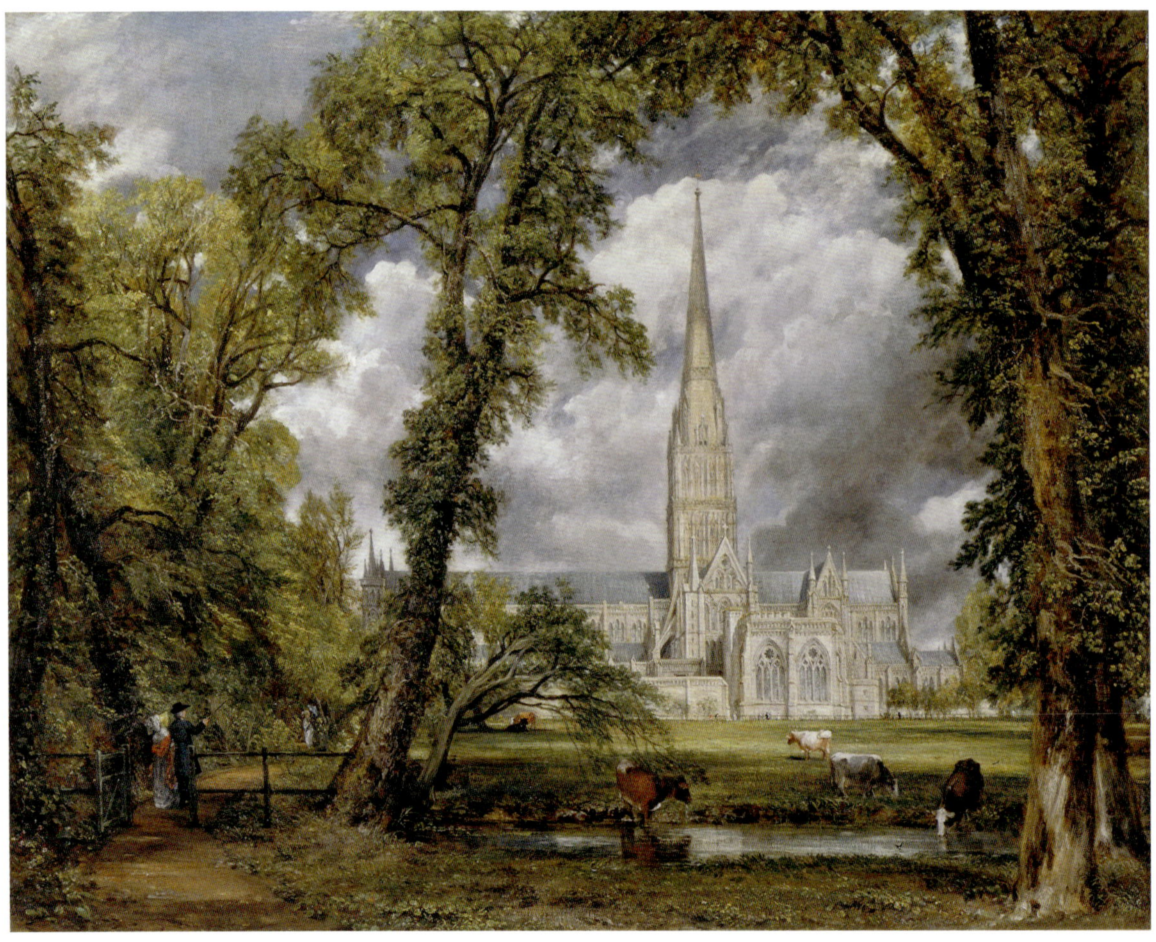

Fig. 31
John Constable
Salisbury Cathedral from the Bishop's Grounds, 1823
Oil on canvas
34½ × 44 in. (87.6 × 111.8 cm)
Victoria and Albert Museum, London; Given by John Sheepshanks, 1857 (FA.333[O])

in Salisbury just before July 1, according to Fisher, "looking very placid & not as if just returned from the continent."[88] With it came the first of several versions of Constable's *Salisbury Cathedral from the Bishop's Grounds* (fig. 31), initially commissioned by Fisher's uncle, the bishop of Salisbury, also called John Fisher. Bishop Fisher—who is depicted with his wife in the painting, at left, looking toward the cathedral—had rejected Constable's first version on account of the dark clouds looming over the cathedral, and Constable, rather than reworking the painting, produced a second version with a brighter sky (fig. 32).[89] The bishop died before Constable completed it. The younger Fisher made mention of receiving, with *The White Horse*, a painting of "the Cathedral" in which the "spire sails away with the thunder-clouds," presumably referring

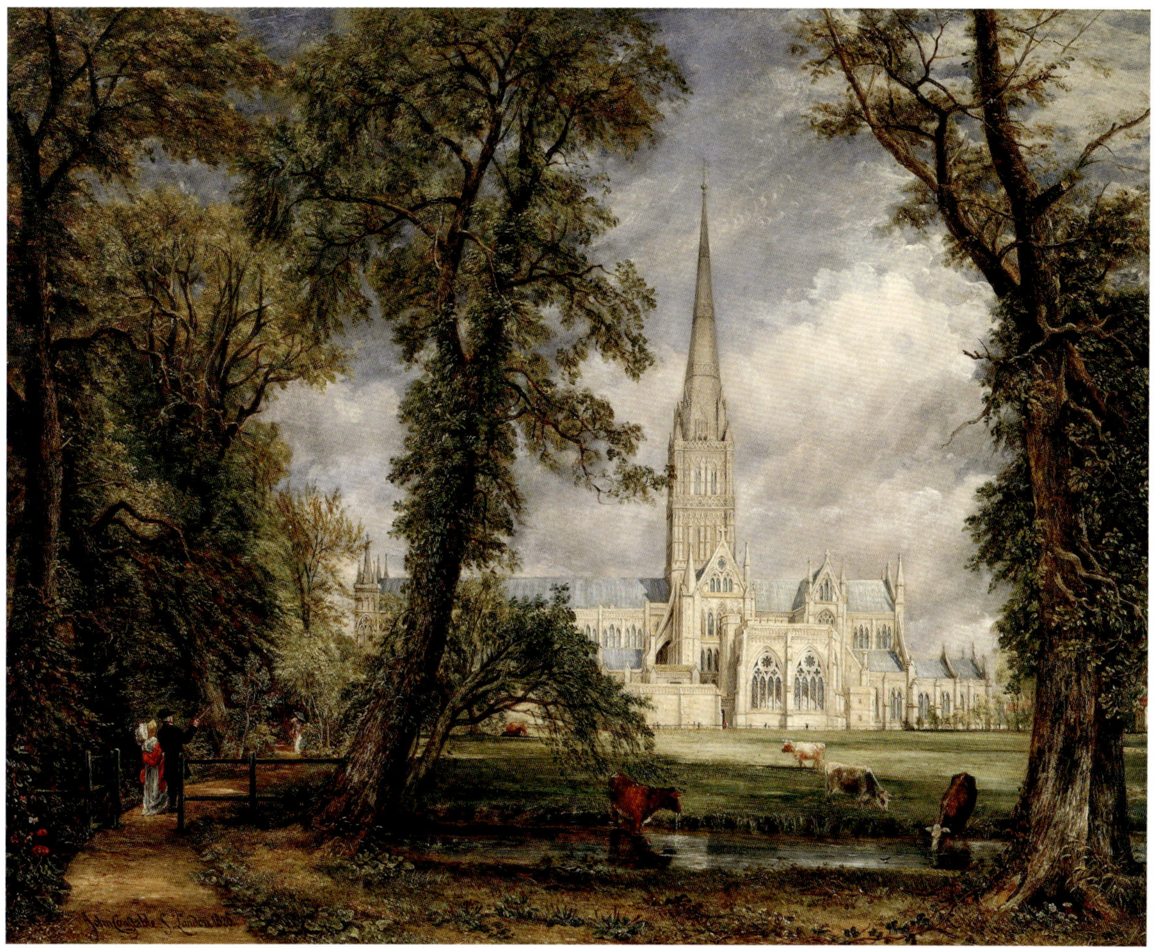

Fig. 32
John Constable
Salisbury Cathedral from the Bishop's Grounds, 1826
Oil on canvas
35 × 44 ¼ in. (88.9 × 112.4 cm)
The Frick Collection, New York; Henry Clay Frick Bequest (1908.1.23)

to his acquisition of the rejected first version, which the bishop's heirs must have relinquished when they accepted the second.[90]

Constable bought *The White Horse* and the first *Salisbury Cathedral from the Bishop's Grounds* back from the struggling younger Fisher in 1830, and he retained both until his death. At the 1838 sale of his studio, *The White Horse* was purchased by Lancelot Archer Burton, husband of Constable's cousin and co-guardian (with the artist's brother, Golding) of Constable's seven children after his death.[91] According to Leslie, Archer Burton refused an offer of 600 guineas for it in the early 1840s.[92] It passed to his son, Burton Archer-Burton, and through several private collections in England; in 1894, it entered the collection of J. Pierpont Morgan, who installed it in his London home, where it remained until 1912, when an exhibition of his paintings was organized in America.

In the summer of 1912, *The White Horse* boarded the S.S. *Majestic* in Southampton, England, for its voyage across the Atlantic.[93] It was one of twenty-nine paintings—packed in seven crates, with *The White Horse* the only one having its own—loaned from the Morgan collection in London for an exhibition at the Metropolitan Museum of Art in New York. The exhibition opened in January 1913. Morgan died in March. His son, J. Pierpont Morgan Jr., known as Jack, arranged for the exhibition of his father's entire collection at the Metropolitan Museum from 1914 to 1916. During this period, in part to satisfy tax liabilities and to keep the estate liquid, Jack sold parts of it to collectors like Henry Clay Frick. Constable's *White Horse*, however, remained in the Morgan collection until Jack's death in 1943.

The painting was purchased by the trustees of The Frick Collection from the Morgan estate, in September 1943, along with four other paintings and a sculpture.[94] It was wartime. In 1942, after the Japanese attack on Pearl Harbor, the most valuable works in the collection were stored for safekeeping in a new vault that had been built at the Frick, underground to the east of the museum building. *The White Horse* went to the vault. At the end of the war, in 1945, the Frick unveiled to great acclaim a new installation of the collection, with the treasures out of the bunker and some additions.[95] Among the new acquisitions on view, *The White Horse* joined in the Frick's galleries another painting by Constable, the second version of *Salisbury Cathedral from the Bishop's Grounds* that Frick had purchased in 1908. Ironically, Constable's *White Horse*—a monument to pre-industrial England—found its home in the Fifth Avenue mansion of Frick, one of the foremost industrialists in the history of the United States.

Notes

1 Delacroix 1854, 309; on Cézanne, see Clark 1946, 12, 15; on Constable as "the single most revolutionary influence on Western painting" of the last nearly two centuries and his influence on Courbet, Manet, and Matisse, see Heron in London, Toronto, and New York 1994–95, 45; Lucian Freud quoted in Paris 2002–3, 61; on Jackson Pollock, see Cove 2006–7, 61.

2 Turner also exhibited *England: Richmond Hill, on the Prince Regent's Birthday*.

3 Constable to Fisher, January 23, 1825, in Constable 1962–70, 6: 191: "My reputation at home among my brother artists [is] dayly gaining ground, & I deeply feel the honour of having found an original style & independent of him who would be Lord over all—I mean Turner."

4 Ibid., 6: 211.

5 Sarah Cove (2006–7, 62) draws attention to this unfinished quality in *Salisbury Cathedral from the Meadows* in her discussion of color change in Constable's later sketches.

6 Constable's journal entry on June 22, 1824, in Constable 1962–70, 4: 184: "I hope not to go to Paris as long as I live."

7 Constable to Fisher on May 9, 1823, in Constable 1962–70, 6: 117: "I was born to paint a happier land, my own dear England." In his second draft for the *English Landscape* publication (with David Lucas; see below), Constable wrote: "Satisfied that these attributes of it are to be met with in perhaps greater perfection in this than in any other country, and also, that the features of this country itself abundantly contain all that is so eagerly sought under foreign skies—he [i.e., himself, the author] would willingly lend his aid towards encreasing [sic] the love, and consequent study of the beauties which lie beneath our own" (Constable 1962–70, 7: 83).

8 The social history of Constable's artistic context was illuminated in the seminal works by Anne Bermingham (1986) and John Barrell (1980). On January 14, 1826, Constable wrote to Fisher: "My brother has had great losses in business—& he can't help me" (Constable 1962–70, 6: 213).

9 Constable to Fisher, April 13, 1822, in Constable 1962–70, 6: 88: "My brother is uncomfortable about the state of things in Suffolk. They are as bad as Ireland—'never a night without seeing fires near or at a distance.' The *Rector* & his brother the *Squire* have forsaken the village—no abatement of tithes or rents—four of Sir William Rush's tenants distrained next parish—these things are ill timed."

10 Constable to Fisher, October 23, 1821, in Constable 1962–70, 6: 78. Constable continues: "They [all that lies on the banks of the Stour] made me a painter (& I am grateful) that is I had often thought of pictures of them before I had ever touched a pencil, and your picture [*The White Horse*] is one of the strongest instances I can recollect of it." Later in life, Constable would emphasize scientific aspects of painting. In his fourth lecture at the Royal Institution, given June 16, 1836, he said, "Painting is a science, and should be pursued as an inquiry into the laws of nature. Why, then, may not landscape be considered as a branch of natural philosophy, of which pictures are but the experiments?" (Constable 1962–70, 7: 69).

11 On the six-footers, see especially London, Washington, and San Marino 2006–7.

12 Fisher first drew attention to the horse in renaming the painting in a letter to Constable, July 2, 1819, in Constable 1962–70, 6: 44: "We will call it if you please '*Life* and the pale Horse,' in contradistinction to Mr. Wests [sic] painting [*Death on the Pale Horse*]." When Fisher received the painting in 1820, he wrote in a letter to Constable, April 27, in Constable 1962–70, 6: 53: "Constable's 'White Horse' has arrived safe." The archdeacon also coined "The Leaping Horse," though his name for *Stratford Mill*—"The Touchwood Tree"—did not catch on (Constable 1962–70, 6: 144).

13 For Robert Hunt's review in *The Examiner*, June 27, 1819, see Ivy 1991, 82: "Of a very different style [than Turner's *Richmond Hill*], though equally successful of its kind, is Mr. Constable's, who though he also is still far from pencilling with Nature's precision, gives her more contracted features, such as a wood or a windmill on a river, with more of her aspect. He does not give a sentiment, a soul to the exterior of Nature, as Mr. Turner does; he does not at all exalt the spectator's mind, which Mr. Turner eminently does, but he gives her outward look, her complexion and physical countenance, with more exactness. He has none of the poetry of nature like Mr. Turner, but he has more of her portraiture. His *Scene on the River Stour* is indeed more approaching to the outward lineament and look of trees, water, boats, &c. than any of our landscape painters. There is perhaps a little inaccuracy in the perspective keeping of the remoter parts." The unsigned

review in *The Literary Gazette*, July 3, 1819, is the first to associate Constable with Ruysdael and Hobbema (ibid., 83).

14 Constable to Fisher, January 14, 1826, in Constable 1962–70, 6: 212: "Your picture did me great credit at Lille. . . . There are generally in the life of an artist, perhaps one, two or three pictures, on which hang more than usual interest—this is mine." Constable called it "one of my happiest efforts on a large scale, being a placid representation of a serene grey morning" (Leslie 1845, 82).

15 London 1825, no. 117 ("Landscape; a River Scene"). The medal (whereabouts unknown; inscribed on the reverse, VILLE DE LILLE/ EXPOSITION/ 1825/ M. CONSTABLE) is first illustrated (without a location) in Leslie (1896, 185), which is a reprint of Leslie's 1843 text, updated and illustrated by his son, Robert Charles Leslie. In 1824, the French king awarded Constable a gold medal (now at the National Gallery, London, History Collection) for his submissions to the Paris Salon: *The Hay Wain* and *View on the Stour near Dedham*. Beckett (in Constable 1962–70, 5: 64) suggests *The White Horse* may have been the painting exhibited in Worcester in 1836 as no. 48, titled *A Farm Yard near a Navigable River in Suffolk* (Constable having given "Farm Yard" as an alternate title in his notes for *English Landscape*; see note 81 below).

16 Fisher to Constable, October 25, 1823, in Constable 1962–70, 6: 142: "Your Tinney picture is down. I have lent him the 'white horse' to hang in its stead." Tinney refused Constable's request to send *Stratford Mill* to an exhibition in Edinburgh.

17 For Fisher's correspondence about the return of the paintings, see Constable 1962–70, 6: 255. Regarding the purchase price, see Constable 1975, 57.

18 See note 91 below on the 1838 Foster's sales catalogues.

19 Rhyne (1990, 129n.65) points out that Constable's largest known canvases are not landscapes but rather two portraits.

20 On Constable's technique, see especially Cove 2006–7.

21 In his diary, Farington (1978–84, 16: 5582) recorded on November 21, 1820 ("my Birth day"): "Constable brought a new begun picture; 'A view on the Thames on the day of opening Waterloo Bridge.' At his request for my opinion I recommended to him to proceed on & complete for the Exhibition a subject more corresponding with his successful picture exhibited last May [*Stratford Mill*]."

22 Constable to Fisher, November 19, 1825, in Constable 1962–70, 6: 207: "My Waterloo like a blister begins to stick closer & closer—& to disturb my nights."

23 According to Leslie (1860, 135), Turner, upon seeing Constable's *Waterloo Bridge* displayed next to his *Helvoetsluys*, "stood behind him, looking from the 'Waterloo' to his own picture, and at last brought his palette from the great room where he was touching another picture, and putting a round daub of red lead, somewhat bigger than a shilling, on his grey sea, went away without saying a word. The intensity of the red lead, made more vivid by the coolness of his picture, caused even the vermillion and lake of Constable to look weak. I [Leslie] came into the room just as Turner left it. 'He has been here,' said Constable, 'and fired a gun.' On the opposite wall was a picture, by Jones, of Shadrach, Meshach, and Abednego in the furnace. 'A coal,' said Cooper, 'has bounced across the room from Jones's picture, and set fire to Turner's sea.' The great man did not come again into the room for a day and a half; and then, in the last moments that were allowed for painting, he glazed the scarlet seal he had put on his picture, and shaped it into a buoy."

24 Constable to Fisher, April 13, 1822, asking for a loan, in Constable 1962–70, 6: 88: "painting these large pictures have much impoverished me." *The White Horse* sold to John Fisher in 1819 for 100 guineas; *Stratford Mill* sold to John Fisher in 1821 as a gift for Tinney for 100 guineas; *The Hay Wain* sold to John Arrowsmith, along with *View on the Stour near Dedham* and *Yarmouth Jetty*, for £250 (equivalent to about 238 guineas); *The Lock* sold in 1824 to James Morrison for 150 guineas; *The Leaping Horse* was likely sold as part of the artist's posthumous sale in 1838 for £52.10s (equivalent to about 50 guineas; see Foster and Sons 1838, lot 35). Vaughan (2002, 49) suggests that the failure to sell *The Leaping Horse* in 1825 put an end to the series.

25 Golding Constable acquired Flatford Mill from his uncle Abram through an inheritance that included stock in trade and shipping, cash, and landed property in East Bergholt (Constable 1962–70, 1: 4–5); he later acquired the corn mill at Dedham and a windmill at East Bergholt (Constable 1962–70, 1: 5, and Rosenthal 1983, 239n.13). Regarding the transport business, including the ship *Telegraph*, which transported corn between Mistley and London and was apparently replaced by *Balloon*, see Cormack 1986, 12, and Constable 1962–70, 1: 135.

26 Ibid., 7.

27 Constable to David Lucas, November 14, 1832, in Shirley 1930, 96: "In the coach yesterday coming from Suffolk—were two gentlemen and myself all strangers to each other—in passing through the Valley about Dedham one of them remarked to me—on my saying it was beautifull [sic]—yes sir—this is *Constable's* country!! I then told him who I was lest he should spoil it."

28 Reynolds (1984, 1: 27), for example, with the aid of Charles Rhyne, corrects the precise location of the scene from that identified in earlier sources: the view is taken "from the right bank of the Stour just below Flatford Lock and looking towards Willy Lott's House," and not between Flatford and Dedham.

29 Leslie (1845, 314) describes in his memoirs of Constable: "We found that Constable had rather combined and varied the materials, than given exact views. In the larger compositions, such as 'The White Horse' and 'The Hay Wain,' both from this neighbourhood, he has increased the width of the river to great advantage; and wherever there was an opportunity, he was fond of introducing the tower of Dedham Church, which is seen from many points near Flatford."

30 For example, Constable refers to painting Willy Lott's Cottage in a letter to John Dunthorne, February 22, 1814, in Constable 1962–70, 1: 101; see Beckett (in ibid., 102) for notes on the cottage.

31 On lighters on the River Stour, see De Salis 1904, 23.

32 Ibid., 4.

33 Lyles (in London, Washington, and San Marino 2006–7, 105) has suggested that the idea for full-size sketches may have come in 1817 when he used a *plein air* sketch as if it were a near same-scale sketch for a more finished painting.

34 In one instance in which Constable may be referring to a full-size sketch for *View on the Stour near Dedham* (Constable to Fisher, April 1, 1822, in Constable 1962–70, 6: 89), he refers to removing a sail from and adding a second barge to the composition. This corresponds to his painting out a sail in the sketch, which can be observed in the X-radiograph; the exhibition painting does not seem to have ever included the deleted sail. He adds a second barge only to the exhibition picture. Thus, he makes no explicit distinction between making changes in the sketch and making changes in the exhibition painting, instead referring only to the composition itself. On the composition, see Lyles in London, Washington, and San Marino 2006–7, 146–51.

35 Leslie 1855, 276. On extant full- or nearly full-size sketches, see the catalogue entries in London, Washington, and San Marino 2006–7.

36 Cove 2006–7, 58–59.

37 Recent examination by X-radiograph shows a few vertical notches along the top edge that are not at regular intervals but possibly relate to squaring with threads after the painting was finished, perhaps in order to make an engraving. My thanks to Charlotte Hale.

38 In 1842 or 1843, Leslie identified obvious forgeries that the brewer of Arundel, George Constable (no relation), had tried to exchange for prints (Constable 1962–70, 4: 177). Moreover, Constable's son Lionel was an artist whose paintings have been mistaken for those of his father; see London 1982.

39 The smaller copy (15¾ × 21½ in.), formerly in the collection of Mr. and Mrs. Herbert L. Satterlee (Mrs. Satterlee being the daughter of J. Pierpont Morgan), last appeared on the market in 2000 at an auction in New York (William Doyle Galleries 2000, lot 84). The other (40½ × 54 in.) was deaccessioned by the Museum of Fine Arts, Boston, in 1992 (Sotheby's 1992, lot 528).

40 My thanks to Jessica David for discussing the *Stratford Mill* sketch and its history with me.

41 The engraving by Jahyer is published in Barnett 1883, 333.

42 London 1872, no. 118. On its provenance, see Hayes 1992, 1942.9.9.

43 Parris and Fleming-Williams 1985, 167.

44 Hoozee 1979, 112–13, no. 618 ("molto probabilmente un'imitazione"). Reynolds (1984, 1: 29–30), however, included it in his catalogue. Franklin Biebel of The Frick Collection, John Walker of the National Gallery of Art, and C. H. Collins Baker of the Huntington Library, in unpublished correspondence in March 1944, discuss the possibility of the National Gallery of Art painting being a sketch for the Frick picture; both museum acquisitions were made around the same time in 1942 (NGA) and 1943 (Frick). Baker seemed particularly prescient in his letter to Frederick Mortimer Clapp, director of the Frick (March 22, 1944): "I should not be surprised if the Widener version is a rough tryout by Constable himself—perhaps on an old, discarded canvas." Copies of the letters are in the Frick curatorial files.

45 See, for example, Rhyne 1990 and Rhyne and Swicklik 1994.

46 Michael Swicklik (1998, 369–70) observed a single layer of paint in an area of clouds at left, a tree at right, and, at the lower left corner, in the vine encircling the post, suggesting these areas were painted in *Dedham Vale* and integrated into *The White Horse*. My thanks to him for discussing with me his recent reconsideration of these areas, especially the vine encircling the post, which appears to be more complex than previously perceived.

47 Ibid., 371.

48 Ibid., 370.

49 My thanks to Charlotte Hale, Conservator, and Evan Read, Associate Manager of Technical Documentation, in the Department of Paintings Conservation at the Metropolitan Museum of Art for undertaking the examination and interpretation and for discussing the results with me.

50 Reynolds 1984, 1: 30; Rhyne 1990, 118; and Parris and Fleming-Williams 1985, 167, debate the nature of the dark form.

51 Thanks to Michael Swicklik for discussing the full-size sketch with me.

52 My thanks to Sarah Cove, ACR, founder of the Constable Research Project, for discussing with me her studies of *The White Horse* and associated works; she recently (correspondence 2020) drew attention to the unusual use of twill weave canvas for the Washington sketch and the vertical oil sketch (fig. 26).

53 Reynolds 1973, 90. Reynolds (1984, 1: 28) suggests a number of other sketches that may relate to the plough and water lilies in *The White Horse*.

54 On the boathouse drawing, see Reynolds 1984, 1: no. 19.5, and New York 1988, no. 67; on the boat drawing, see Cormack 1986, 128.

55 On the vertical oil sketch (fig. 26), see Reynolds 1984, 1: no. 19.3, and Sotheby's 2019, lot 23. On the horizontal sketch (fig. 27), see Reynolds 1984, 1: no. 19.4; London 1976, no. 165; and Sotheby's 2019, lot 20A. Regarding the latter, Sarah Cove (correspondence 2020) has dated the horizontal sketch to the summer of 1816 on the basis of the use of a dark chocolate brown ground, found only in works produced in this year; my thanks to her for discussing this with me. On the barge oil sketch (fig. 28), discovered in 2004 (see Bonhams 2004, lot 364, as "British School (19thc)") and first published in London, Washington, and San Marino 2006–7, 133, see Sotheby's 2009, lot 26.

56 On Constable's composing, see, especially, Cove 2006–7, 58.

57 Taylor 1973, 38.

58 Leslie 1845, 105.

59 Reynolds 1984, 1: 1–3.

60 He made significant changes to *The Leaping Horse*, for example, after exhibiting it in 1825; see Lyles in London, Washington, and San Marino 2006–7, 156–58.

61 Constable to an unknown correspondent, dated March 8 (year unknown), in Constable 1962–70, 4: 129: "It is much to my advantage that several of my pictures should be seen together, as it displays to an advantage their varieties of conception and also of execution, and what they gain by the mellowing hand of time, which should never be forced or anticipated." He addresses the effect of air and time on his paints in a letter to Fisher of April 13, 1825, in Constable 1962–70, 6: 200: "My Lock is now on my easel. It looks most beautifully silvery, windy & delicious—it is all health—& the absence of every thing stagnant, and is wonderfully got together after only this one year." He wrote about humidity in a letter to Fisher, October 21, 1822, in Constable 1962–70, 6: 100: "I have got this room (the large painting room) into excellent order. It is light—airy—*sweet* & warm. I at one time despaired of attaining either of these qualities, especially the latter, but we discovered a real grievance—a hollow wall—which communicated with the floors of my room, opened & was immediately over—the *well* of the *privy*. This would have played the devil with the oxygen of my colours." On change in Constable's pigments, see Cove 2006–7, 65.

62 For example, in 1814 a writer in *The Examiner* criticized Constable's *Ferry* as "deficient in finishing" (Ivy 1991, 69). In a letter to John Dunthorne, February 22, 1814, in Constable 1962–70, 1: 101, Constable refers to making small sketches on site to help with the finishing of his large landscapes. On Constable and finish, see also Cove 2006–7, 62–67.

63 Fisher to Constable, October 2, 1823, in Constable 1962–70, 6: 134–35: "He [Tinney] dreads your touching the picture. This of course is not his own thought, for he would not discover any alteration you might make. But it is the suggestions of Lewis the engraver. 'There is a look of nature about the picture,'

says Lewis, 'which seems as if it were introduced by magic. This, when Constable gets it on his easil [sic], he may in an unlucky moment destroy: and he will never paint another picture like it, for he has unfortunately taken to copy himself.' You must take the sweet & the bitter together. Lewis seemed to speak, Tinney said, as if he reported the opinion of other artists as well as himself. I leave you to digest the criticism as you may. If it is just, it is right you should know it: if it is erroneous it will put you on your guard."

64 As noted above, Tinney reluctantly sent *Stratford Mill* to the Paris Salon in 1824 and refused to send it to Edinburgh the following year.

65 Fisher to Constable, June 6, 1819, in Constable 1962–70, 6: 44: "Did you not express a wish to have it on your easil [sic] again to subdue a few lights and cool your trees? I think you said so. Because the gentleman who meditates the purchase does not immediately want it."

66 The "ARA" is difficult to see and has been omitted from transcriptions of the inscription (e.g., Reynolds 1984, 1: 27, and repeated in London, Washington, and San Marino 2006–7, 135); technical examination confirms its presence. In Reynolds 1984, 1: 27, the letters "IC" preceding "John Constable" were recorded (and suggested to represent a first and less complete signature), but these were not detected in recent examination.

67 Inscriptions on Constable's paintings are not always easy to decipher. According to the inscriptions transcribed by Reynolds from 1802 to 1819, no other work bears the name of a place that it does not purportedly depict.

68 Rosenthal 1983, 117.

69 Reynolds (1984, 1: no. 19.6) suggested the drawing may have been made to frame a smaller copy, citing Rhyne's attribution of the ex-MFA copy to Constable's assistant John Dunthorne; see Rhyne's lecture given at the annual meeting of the College Art Association, February 17, 1994, New York City (https://www.reed.edu/art/rhyne/papers/deaccessioning.html, accessed January 14, 2020). Gadney (1976, no. 25) discusses the framers known to have been associated with Constable.

70 Reynolds 1984, 1: 31.

71 Constable to Fisher, December 17, 1824, in Constable 1962–70, 6: 186.

72 Fisher to Constable, July 1, 1826, in Constable 1962–70, 6: 221–22: "The two pictures arrived safe on Friday, & within an hour were up in their places; the white horse looking very placid & not as if just returned from the continent. It is wonderfully improved by Dunthorne's coat of varnish."

73 Fisher to Constable, July 1, 1826, in Constable 1962–70, 6: 222. Fisher received *The White Horse* along with a version of *Salisbury Cathedral from the Bishop's Grounds*, and he refers to sending back the old frame and a smaller packing case.

74 Constable to Fisher, July 17, 1819, in Constable 1962–70, 6: 45: "The price I have fixed upon my large landscape is 100 Guineas exclusive of the frame."

75 Reynolds (1984, 1: 29) suggests that Constable made an outline study of some of the main features of *The White Horse*, which developed a new series of works.

76 On the uncertainty regarding the precise date of the origination of the project, see Constable 1962–70, 4: 319.

77 Delacroix wrote in his journal in 1846 (Delacroix 2009, 2: 1652–53): "Constable dit que la supériorité du vert de ses prairies tient à ce qu'il est composé d'une multitude de verts différents. Ce qui donne le défaut d'intensité et de vie à la verdure du commun des paysagistes, c'est qu'ils la font ordinairement d'une teinte uniforme. Ce qu'il dit ici du vert des prairies peut s'appliquer à tous les autres tons" (Constable says that the superiority of the green of his meadows is due to its being composed of a multitude of different greens. That which gives the lack of intensity and life in the greenery of ordinary landscapists is that they usually make it with a uniform shade. What he says here of the green of his meadows can be applied to all other tones).

78 See Constable 1962–70, 4: 318, and Constable's notes on the proofs in ibid., Appendix C. In a 1994 lecture, Rhyne emphasized the collaborative authorship of the prints and their proofs (see note 69).

79 Constable to Lucas, September 15, 1829, in Constable 1962–70, 4: 322. Constable instructs Lucas to come to take a number of landscapes away (from Constable's studio to his own, nearby) to begin translating them into prints. For larger works, the messenger Holland was presumably sent to collect them (see letter from Constable to Lucas, August 1831, in Constable 1962–70, 4: 353: "Send by Holland what you have that you wish to be no longer lumbered with").

80 Shirley 1930, 180.

81 Constable 1962–70, 4: Appendices A, X.

82 Constable to Lucas, October 7, 1832, in Constable 1962–70, 4: 382: "Perhaps it will be as well to re-engrave on a new plate the 'White Horse' or substitute it for another."

83 Constable to Lucas, June 27, 1833, in Constable 1962–70, 4: 401.

84 Constable 1962–70, 4: 439.

85 Shirley 1930, 180.

86 Constable in London to Fisher, January 14, 1826, in Constable 1962–70, 6: 212. According to Beckett (ibid., 212n.3), the pictures had been consigned from Calais on December 28, 1825, to a Captain Margollé, master of the *Perseverance*, and the bills of lading were preserved in the Plymouth Collection.

87 Constable 1962–70, 6: 212n.3. Beckett suggested the reference to two paintings may have been a slip; elsewhere, Beckett proposed the second might be *Stratford Mill* (Constable 1962–70, 4: 273): "The use of the plural in the first sentence is strange, when only one picture belonging to Fisher had in fact been sent to Lille. There might be a possible explanation, however, if the exhibits had included *Stratford Mill*, which Fisher had purchased and then given to his solicitor, J. P. Tinney, and to which Constable proceeds to refer."

88 Constable 1962–70, 6: 221–22.

89 Bishop Fisher died in 1825, and Constable gave the painting to his heirs in February of 1826; see Constable 1962–70, 6: 213.

90 Fisher to Constable, July 1, 1826, in Constable 1962–70, 6: 222.

91 In the copy of the 1838 Foster and Sons sale catalogue (*A Catalogue of the valuable finished works, studies and sketches of John Constable, Esq. R.A. deceased*) in the Frick Art Reference Library, the name "Morton" that appears next to lot 77 ("View of the River Stour, with White Horse in a Barge") is presumably an error and is one of several discrepancies with the copy in the National Art Library at the Victoria and Albert Museum, which gives the buyer as "Burton" (and sale prices in both guineas and pounds; *The White Horse* sold for 150 guineas, or £157.10s). Thanks to Mark Evans for discussing the sales catalogues with me. According to Parris and Fleming-Williams (1985, 167), the painting passed from Lancelot Archer Burton to his son Burton Archer-Burton, who was the unnamed vendor in the 1855 Christie's sale (lot 99). On Lancelot Archer Burton, see Fleming-Williams and Parris 1984, 4. *The White Horse* was purchased by Hodgson for 600 guineas; then was with Richard Hemming; was purchased from Mrs. Hemming's estate in 1894 by Agnews for 6,200 guineas; and J. Pierpont Morgan purchased it from Agnews for £6,835.10s (equivalent to about 6,510 guineas) on May 7, 1894 (see Agnews, Picture Stock Book, 1891–1898, entry 6852). My thanks to Zara Moran for her assistance with the Agnews archives.

92 C. R. Leslie to Francis Darby, May 22, 1843, in Constable 1975, 248: "I am not sure which picture of the Stour valley it was, which you say he sent to Worcester about ten years ago.—If the 'White Horse', which is certainly one of his finest works, it is now in the possession of Mr. Archer Burton, of Hants, who has lately, I am told, refused 600 guineas for it."

93 I thank Jennifer Tonkovich for her help regarding the Morgan collection.

94 Rembrandt's *Nicolas Ruts*, Goya's *Duke of Osuna*, Greuze's *Woolwinder*, Reynolds's *General John Burgoyne*, and Jean Barbet's *Angel* were acquired with *The White Horse* for a total of $495,000, most of which was for the Barbet *Angel* ($250,000). Held at Knoedler's galleries on 57th Street in New York, *The White Horse* visited the Frick on approval for just under a week in September of 1943. My thanks to Susan Chore and colleagues in the Archives Department at the Frick for their help with the Frick archives.

95 *New York Herald Tribune*, May 5, 1945, "Frick Paintings Removed From War Hide-Away."

BIBLIOGRAPHY

Barnett 1883 Barnett, Harry V. "The 'White Horse': A Note on Constable." *Magazine of Art* 6 (1883): 333–35.

Barrell 1980 Barrell, John. *The Dark Side of the Landscape: The Rural Poor in English Painting, 1730–1840*. Cambridge: Cambridge University Press, 1980.

Bermingham 1986 Bermingham, Ann. *Landscape and Ideology: The English Rustic Tradition, 1740–1850*. Berkeley: University of California, 1986.

Bonhams 2004 *Art and Antiquities Sale*. Sale cat. Bonhams Edinburgh, April 22, 2004.

Chicago 1946 *Masterpieces of English Painting: William Hogarth, John Constable, J.M.W. Turner*. Exh. cat. Chicago (Art Institute of Chicago), 1946.

Clark 1946 Clark, Kenneth. "Hogarth, Constable, and Turner." In Chicago 1946, 9–16.

Constable 1962–70 Constable, John. *John Constable's Correspondence*. Edited by R. B. Beckett. 7 vols. Ipswich: Suffolk Records Society, 1962–70.

Constable 1975 Constable, John. *John Constable: Further Documents and Correspondence*. Edited by Leslie Parris and Conal Shields. London: Tate Gallery, 1975.

Cormack 1986 Cormack, Malcolm. *Constable*. Oxford: Phaidon Press, 1986.

Cove 2006–7 Cove, Sarah. "The Painting Techniques of John Constable's 'Six-Footers.'" In London, Washington, and San Marino 2006–7, 50–69.

Delacroix 1854 Delacroix, Eugène. "Questions sur le Beau." *Revue des Deux Mondes* 2 (1854): 306–15.

Delacroix 2009 Delacroix, Eugène. *Journal 1822–1857*. 2 vols. Paris: José Corti, 2009.

De Salis 1904 De Salis, Henry Rodolph. *Bradshaw's Canals and Navigable Rivers of England and Wales*. London: Henry Black & Co. Ltd., 1904.

Farington 1978–84 Farington, Joseph. *The Diary of Joseph Farington*. Edited by Kenneth Garlick and Angus Macintyre. 16 vols. New Haven: Yale University Press, 1978–84.

Fleming-Williams and Parris 1984 Fleming-Williams, Ian, and Leslie Parris. *The Discovery of Constable*. London: Hamish Hamilton, 1984.

Foster and Sons 1838 *A Catalogue of the valuable finished works, studies and sketches of John Constable, Esq. R.A. deceased*. Sale cat. Messrs. Foster and Sons, London, May 15–16, 1838.

Gadney 1976 Gadney, Reg. *John Constable R.A. 1776–1837. A Catalogue of Drawings and Watercolors, with a selection of Mezzotints by David Lucas, after Constable for 'English Landscape Scenery,' in the Fitzwilliam Museum, Cambridge*. London: Arts Council of Great Britain, 1976.

Hayes 1992 Hayes, John. *British Paintings of the Sixteenth through Nineteenth Centuries*. Washington: National Gallery of Art, 1992.

Hoozee 1979 Hoozee, Robert. *L'Opera completa di Constable*. Milan: Rizzoli Editore, 1979.

Ivy 1991 Ivy, Judy C. *Constable and the Critics: 1802–1837*. Woodbridge, Suffolk, and Rochester, N.Y.: Boydell in association with the Suffolk Records Society, 1991.

Leslie 1845 Leslie, Charles Robert. *Memoirs of the Life of John Constable, R.A.: Composed Chiefly of His Letters*. 2nd ed. London: Longman, Brown, Green, and Longmans, 1845.

Leslie 1855 Leslie, Charles Robert. *A Handbook for Young Painters*. London: John Murray, 1855.

Leslie 1860 Leslie, Charles Robert. *Autobiographical Recollections*. Boston: Ticknor and Fields, 1860.

Leslie 1896 Leslie, Charles Robert. *Life and Letters of John Constable, R.A.* London: Chapman and Hall, 1896.

London 1825 *Collection of the Works of Living British Artists*. Exh. cat. London (British Institution), 1825.

London 1872 *Exhibition of the Works of the Old Masters together with Works of Deceased Masters of the British School*. Exh. cat. London (Royal Academy), 1872.

London 1874 *International Exhibition of 1874*. Exh. cat. London (South Kensington Museum), 1874.

London 1976 Leslie Parris. *Constable: Paintings, Watercolours & Drawings*. Exh. cat. London (Tate Gallery), 1976.

London 1982 Leslie Parris. *Lionel Constable*. Exh. cat. London (Tate Gallery), 1982.

London, Toronto, and New York 1994–95 Ian Fleming-Williams. *Constable: A Master Draughtsman*. Exh. cat. London (Dulwich Picture Gallery), Toronto (Art Gallery of Ontario), and New York (The Frick Collection), 1994–95.

London, Washington, and San Marino 2006–7 Anne Lyles, ed. *Constable: The Great Landscapes*. Exh. cat. London (Tate Britain), Washington (National Gallery of Art), and San Marino (Huntington Art Gallery), 2006–7.

New York 1988 Graham Reynolds, Charles Rhyne, and Julius Meier-Graefe. *John Constable, R.A. (1776–1837)*. Exh. cat. New York (Salander-O'Reilly Galleries, Inc.), 1988.

Paris 2002–3 Lucian Freud. *Lucian Freud on John Constable*. Exh. cat. Paris (Grand Palais), 2002–3.

Parris and Fleming-Williams 1985 Parris, Leslie, and Ian Fleming-Williams. Review of *The Later Paintings and Drawings of John Constable*, by Graham Reynolds. *Burlington Magazine* 127, no. 984 (March 1985): 162, 164–70.

Reynolds 1973 Reynolds, Graham. *Catalogue of the Constable Collection*. London: H.M. Stationery Office, 1973.

Reynolds 1984 Reynolds, Graham. *The Later Paintings and Drawings of John Constable*. 2 vols. New Haven and London: Yale University Press, 1984.

Rhyne 1990 Rhyne, Charles. "Constable's First Two Six-Foot Landscapes." *Studies in the History of Art* 24 (1990): 109–29.

Rhyne and Swicklik 1994 Rhyne, Charles, and Michael Swicklik. "Intent in Constable's Full-Size Sketch for *The White Horse*." Preprint, submitted at the American Institute for Conservation 22nd Annual Meeting, Nashville, Tenn., June 6–11, 1994.

Rosenthal 1983 Rosenthal, Michael. *Constable: The Painter and His Landscape*. New Haven: Yale University Press, 1983.

Shirley 1930 Shirley, Andrew. *The Published Mezzotints of David Lucas after John Constable R.A.: A Catalogue and Historical Account.* Oxford: Clarendon Press, 1930.

Sotheby's 1992 *Old Master and 19th Century European Paintings and Drawings*. Sale cat. Sotheby's New York, July 16, 1992.

Sotheby's 2009 *Early British Paintings*. Sale cat. Sotheby's London, July 9, 2009.

Sotheby's 2019 *Old Masters Evening Sale*. Sale cat. Sotheby's London, July 3, 2019.

Swicklik 1998 Swicklik, Michael. "Interpreting Artist's Intent in the Treatment of John Constable's *The White Horse* Sketch." *Journal of the American Institute for Conservation* 37 (1998): 362–72.

Taylor 1973 Taylor, Basil. *Constable: Paintings, Drawings, and Watercolours*. London: Phaidon, 1973.

Vaughan 2002 Vaughan, William. *John Constable*. London: Tate Publishing, 2002.

William Doyle Galleries 2000 *Important English and Continental Furniture and Decorations*. Sale cat. William Doyle Galleries, New York, May 17, 2000.

INDEX

Page numbers in *italics* refer to the illustrations.

IMAGE CREDITS

Photographs in this book have been provided by the owners or custodians of the works. The following list applies to those photographs for which a separate credit is due.

Figs. 3, 15, 19, 22; pages 2, 6, 8, 10, 24 Joseph Coscia Jr.

Figs. 1, 12, 16 © Tate

Figs. 2, 30, 32 Michael Bodycomb

Figs. 6, 7 © The National Gallery, London

Fig. 9 © Huntington Art Museum, San Marino, California

Fig. 10 Private collection / Bridgeman Images

Fig. 11 © Royal Academy of Arts, London; photo Prudence Cuming Associates Ltd

Fig. 13 Bridgeman Images

Figs. 14, 18, 31 © Victoria and Albert Museum, London

Fig. 23 Department of Paintings Conservation, The Metropolitan Museum of Art

Fig. 29 © Fitzwilliam Museum, Cambridge